"Most of us live our lives in the cramped, shame-filled spaces inside the walls of religious 'shoulds' instead of the liberating freedom of true life in God. Through her own captivating and poignant spiritual autobiography, Gotthardt not only invites us into her experience but also dares us to imagine how God might be calling us to leap into the freedom of faith too. A hilarious, heart-aching, and captivating story, the deep beauty and truth of Gotthardt's journey reminds us all that coming to discover our own true selves, the women and men God uniquely created us to be, can seem downright rebellious."

—Dr. Eric Magnusson, Spring Arbor University

"Kelli's story is not extraordinarily unique; it's a story with which many can relate . . . quietly. What's extraordinary is her courage to take the risk and write about it so openly. Raw, honest, witty, she's not only given a voice to the quiet struggles of many but also a ton of hope that there's a way out. A compelling testimony to the truth that everything is redemptive. What a gift!"

—Wil Hernandez, founder and president of CenterQuest (www.cqcenterquest.org)

"From the earliest pages I was captivated by Kelli's journey, and then it became not only about following someone else's story but an invitation to step into my own. I found myself needing to set the book down, to explore what was there for me, personal to me, and where God was calling me through the brave and generous honesty of Kelli's story. This is about a rebellion not simply for the sake of challenging the status quo but for the purpose of bringing you closer to God, into truer intimacy and terrifyingly surrendered obedience."

—**Sarah Zacharias Davis, executive director of RZIM, and author of** *The Friends We Keep*

"Reading *Unlikely Rebel* is like a personal invitation to curl up with a cup of coffee and have a heart-to-heart with God about the deepest things you feel but never say out loud!"

—**Teresa Goines, 2013 CNN Hero and founder/CEO of Old Skool Cafe**

"I was hooked immediately by Kelli's story and her ability to communicate clearly how devastating and powerful our false beliefs can be and how beautifully redemptive is the message of the gospel. . . . May we all become unlikely rebels who invite others to live out these truths that set hearts free."

—**Shelley Hendrix, founder of Church 4 Chicks, and author of** *Why Can't We Just Get Along?*

"The path of a rebel is as unique as each individual traveler. Ambush and disapproval are to be expected. Kelli Gotthardt's memoir captures the perfect mix of pushing societal boundaries and walking in step with the Spirit."

—**Shirin Tabor, author of** *Wanting All the Right Things* **and** *Muslims Next Door*

"I wish there were more honest stories like this being told, to reclaim the beauty of the church and what it means to follow Jesus."

—**Dan Kimball, Vintage Faith Church, and author of** *They Like Jesus but Not the Church*

"If you've ever struggled with following God versus following what everyone else thinks it means to follow God, you'll relate to Kelli Gotthardt's story. Honest, soul-searching, and still-in-progress, Kelli shares her journey to freedom and invites us to begin our own by considering just how—and where—God is actually leading us to follow."

—Elisa Morgan, speaker, cohost of *Discover the Word*
(discovertheword.org), and author of *The Beauty of Broken*

"A vulnerable testimony to how God can work in painful and embarrassing situations, this book can encourage us as Christ-followers to talk about these issues instead of hiding them or condemning others with them, ultimately achieving deeper healing throughout the church."

—Valerie Hess, author of *A Spiritual Disciplines Devotional*,
and retreat speaker

"Kelli shares beautifully, from her own experience, how she crashed into stillness and found freedom from a faith driven by 'shoulds' and shame. Her story and transparency invite us to consider: What motivates me? Who does God say that I am? I believe this will be a timely read for many. I know it was for me."

—Rachel Triske, executive director of Life in Deep Ellum

"In an honest, kind, and winsome manner, Kelli offers her confessions. What a beautiful story. This book will set people free. If you're tired of trying, and ready for deeper intimacy with God, then this is the book for you."

—Nathan Foster, author of *The Making of an Ordinary Saint*

"This is a book about freedom. Freedom from should and shame. Freedom from the box we often find ourselves trying to fit into. Kelli Gotthardt writes courageously of her quest to live in the freedom and abundant love promised to us by Jesus. I believe her story grants permission to all those on the journey to let go and return to the simplicity of the Father's grace."

—Nancy Beach, leadership coach with the Slingshotgroup,
and author of *Gifted to Lead*

KELLI GOTTHARDT

Unlikely Rebel

A Church Girl's Journey
out of
Shoulds and Shame

Printed in the United States of America
15 16 17 18 19 20 21 22 23 24 / 5 4 3 2 1

To Richard—
whose love has made me a better woman
than I believed I could be

CONTENTS

ACKNOWLEDGMENTS

The following individuals played such a valuable role in the process of my writing that this brief mention seems almost insulting. It will have to do. My publisher has given me a limited numbers of words so I have to use them judiciously.

I have dedicated this book to my husband, Richard, but that brief sentiment doesn't do justice to the journey this was for us as a couple. A number of the following chapters spurred difficult discussions that required long hours to resolve.

Richard, I'm humbled by your willingness to entrust me with telling this story in which you play a prominent role. The reader is getting snapshots of you from my point of view. I hope you share your side of this story someday soon. Through all of this, you have been my biggest fan and encourager, and I know that whatever anyone else thinks about me or my telling of this part of my journey, your love will not waver. I am safe with you.

To my children, Caleb, Cade, and Madison. Because this information is public, I shared details of my life with you that might have otherwise remained unspoken. Not as a secret, but as unnecessary for your journey. That's no longer an option, and you have responded with grace and honesty to this deeper revelation of who I am. We have erred on the side of transparency in our home, and I pray you will continue to lean into the freedom of authenticity and telling the whole truth.

To my parents, Jim and Shirley Kredit, who have always told me how much they love me and have sacrificed financially and emotionally to ensure I was healthy and whole.

To my aunts, Carol DeVelder and Donna Boschma. Without your

prayers and support, I don't know where my story would have ended up. And you didn't stop there. From providing a safe outlet for my adolescent angst to taking me into your home at the height of my unhealthiness, you have both shaped me.

To Carol Travilla, who has shared more wisdom with me than I could ever hope to apply. You have always loved me right where I am and never pushed me to change. Your patience and unconditional love continue to sharpen me. You coached me through most of the transitions of my adult life and taught me how to live the "with-God life." And it was you who first introduced me to the power of my story.

To Matt Smay, who encouraged me to write my story and forged the early connections that made this possible.

To Anna Oatman, who let me use her home like my personal writing retreat. Your friendship and support opened up the time and space for me to pursue this new path.

To Amy Smith, who performed the tedious task of editing my grammar, punctuation, and syntax. You are a true friend. Thanks for always telling me the truth and lovingly taking this text and making it so much better.

To Kendra Roberts, Heidi Blomberg, Rachel Marchessault, Christianne Squires, and Chadwick and Amy Walenga, who read my manuscript at different stages of development and gave me courage to keep going when I most doubted myself.

To my "team of experts"—Soozi Bolte, Jason Kolber, Stephanie Mancuso, Debra Asis, and Joan Webb—who have surrounded me with love and advice, healing and truth, tough love and hugs.

To Alice Crider, my agent, and the team at WordServe. Your belief in the value of my story and your affirmation of who I am have strengthened and encouraged me.

INTRODUCTION:
RULE-BREAKING OBEDIENCE

My mother says I was a compliant child. As a typical firstborn, I lived to obey. More accurately, I lived to avoid the pain of disapproval. I was able to glide through my first twenty years of life squeaky clean. Sure, there were little bumps in the road here and there, but with each bump I was soon back on course, following the rules and making everyone happy.

Ironically, my propensity for following the rules was the very thing keeping me from deeper obedience to God. The emotion-stuffing, impulse-restricting vice of the "good girl" can appear as innocuous clothing, yet disguise a hidden wardrobe of shame and fear.

Then I learned to break the rules. I broke free from enslavement to the expectations of others.

This kind of rule-breaking rebellion looks different than you might think. I didn't get a tattoo (although I haven't ruled it out). I didn't leave my family or my church or change my Gap-inspired monochromatic wardrobe. Plenty of people around me remain unaware of my journey and, to this day, attribute the good things in my life, including my spiritual vibrancy, to strict compliance to the rules. That's too bad, and not the truth.

Which is why I've decided to share a portion of my journey. I've dealt with issues surrounding physical and mental health, faith, abuse, addiction, motherhood, marriage, and depression, all while managing to keep up appearances and follow the rules. Until I learned a new way.

The Rules for Breaking the Rules

It's important to note that I did not set out to be a rebel. And I did not travel this road alone. My goal was to follow Jesus more faithfully, with more joy and more abandon, and this is where he led me. I surrounded myself with a community of fellow travelers who loved me through my wrestling. They helped keep me from needlessly offending too many people or retreating back to the safety of conformity. And along the way I found the Bible and thousands of years of church history littered with stories of similar-hearted rebels.

The challenge with breaking the rules, however, is discerning which rules to break and when. Once you leave the comfort of blind compliance and take responsibility for your own obedience to God, you will find the road quite perilous. It is impossible to do it perfectly, and imperfection is something a good girl hates.

The Benefits of Breaking the Rules

My rebel journey has been a most valuable and life-giving adventure. One that continues to progress with unforeseen twists, perilous landslides, and unparalleled views.

On the way, I've fallen in love with Jesus in ways I never imagined I would. I've discovered rhythms and disciplines that help me connect more deeply with God, and I've attached myself to a community of others who are further along than I. The lingering effects of being assaulted as a teen are subsiding, and I'm no longer a slave to addiction. On many days I like who I am. My capacity to love God and other people continues to grow. I have learned a regular prayer practice that is creative and sometimes vibrant. I enjoy meditating on Scripture and often hear God speaking to me in the Bible's pages.

But I have not arrived.

One other thing I've learned is there are no guarantees of the outcome. The biblical story of Esther describes two rule-breaking women who fell upon drastically different fates. Esther is exceedingly compliant to her uncle Mordecai. So compliant, she agrees to have sex with the king as an audition to be queen. When Mordecai suggests she break the rules and appear before the king without an invitation, she hesitates, knowing this offense is punishable by death. Ultimately she complies. Trusting this is God's plan for her, she bravely proclaims, "If I perish, I perish." Inspirational.

Her predecessor, Queen Vashti, was also a rule breaker. She refused to appear before her drunken husband and be objectified in front of his drunken friends. Seems reasonable. Only it cost her marriage, her position, and her influence. After the men sobered up, they realized that if the queen was allowed to refuse the summons of the king, it could set a bad precedent. They decided to send a message to any other woman who might think she could tell her husband no. They deposed her and promptly set up auditions for a more compliant successor. Not so inspirational.

My Unfinished Story

I should warn you that I am not an expert in anything—even my own story. My perspectives and memories are tainted by my biases, wounds, and humanness. As much as I've attempted to accurately recount key events, I know memory can be an unreliable historian. I have sometimes changed people's names and occasional details have been omitted to protect the privacy of those whose paths have intersected with mine.

These pages document portions of my life in the midst of the journey. If all goes well, I'll read this book in five years and cringe. The insights and freedoms that appear monumental today will hopefully seem elementary in relation to what God has shown me since I pressed *send* on my computer and ceased editing and crafting.

For this reason you may find yourself wondering if I'm qualified to write a spiritual memoir. Shouldn't these books be written by people who are a bit more put together? Probably. But this is what I have to offer, and I hope you may recognize parts of your own journey in mine and that in your journey God might meet you there.

I still wonder if I have published too early. The answer is yes, if my goal is to point you to a conclusion. But after a lengthy period of overanalyzing, I've realized this is not my purpose. Instead, I hope to share with you the beauty and the mess of the long, slow work of God. This is my story in the midst of the transformation.

Don't get me wrong; these are not fresh wounds for which I've only begun the healing process. This is a journey that began nearly thirty years ago and I've been diligent to do the difficult work of living in and working through the pain caused by others and the pain I have caused. But let me say it again—I have not arrived.

When I began the healing journey I was willing to commit a couple of years to pursuing health and holiness so I could get on with my life. Instead, I found a new way of living. On this path I have experienced more freedom and joy than I believed possible or dared hope for. And while I have come to accept the elusive reality of complete wholeness in this life, I am learning to dance in the approving smile of the God who loves me. Where shoulds and shame have less and less power.

But this kind of life is a battle. It's often easier to settle for a safe life of mild spiritual discontentment that keeps us busy with virtuous activity. So this road is not for those who cling to a spiritual formula promising safe travel and a predetermined outcome. The path of the rebel is as unique as each individual traveler. Danger and ambush are to be expected.

This journey is also not for the dissenter who fancies freedom without accountability or growth without pain. Discipline, perseverance, and a willingness to submit are topmost on the job description of a rule-breaking follower of Jesus.

Rule followers are asked to lay down the security of their rules, and rebels are asked to learn obedience.

Notes on Reading This Book

This book is not a manual but a journal. I've organized it into three movements: Leaning In, Letting Go, and Living Out. These are the large categories from which my journey has emerged but they overlap in more of an ever-widening circle than a sequential path. The first section chronicles the series of events that started me on this road, but the second section jumps around chronologically because life is messy and transformation takes a long time. The third section falls back into more of a linear sequence. You're smart. You'll figure it out.

As I've written, I've prayed. I've prayed that my story would not simply be more noise. I've pondered what kind of person writes a book about herself. But ultimately I believe there is power in story. There has been healing in me as I've recounted it. And at the very least, you can celebrate with me as you see redemption unfold. But I pray that God may reveal more of himself to you as you enter into this sacred space with me. I don't know what you will discover as you read, but I have found that as I chose to let go of the shoulds and the shame that kept me cowering under an onerous weight, I found a terrifying and beautiful place where Love dwells. And I have never looked back.

May you discover this same Love.

Leaning In

An efficiently busy life that keeps us occupied without
being harried and keeps our attention entirely on
interesting outer things is probably more potentially
destructive of spiritual growth than debauchery
or alcohol or hard drugs.

—Morton Kelsey

This is what the Sovereign Lord, the Holy One of
Israel, says: "In repentance and rest is your salvation,
in quietness and trust is your strength,
but you would have none of it."

—Isaiah 30:15

CHAPTER 1

The Beautiful No

I felt the tension come in waves washing over my entire body. My husband, Richard, and I were sitting two feet from each other in the car, but the distance was growing rapidly. I had just announced to him my resignation from the litany of volunteer ministry roles I'd accumulated under his pastoral leadership over the past ten years.

I hadn't been coerced into saying yes to all these things. I had simply let life happen to me. But underneath the put-together exterior, I felt my soul shrinking and an internal storm brewing. Unfortunately for Richard, one of the truths of marriage is there are no isolated storms. My storm was now his storm, and in an instant I had altered the fabric of our marriage.

I focused my gaze straight ahead in an effort to keep from losing my nerve. "I'm done with ministry," I said again and with a greater effort to hold back tears. My lungs were failing me as I attempted in vain to take a slow, deep breath.

"Just like that? No discussion? You're just out?" He had no category under which to process this new revelation. There had been no warning, no outward signs of distress. Surely, he believed he had misunderstood me.

"I guess." My mind was reeling and my resolve fading. "Not forever. Just for the next year. I need to regroup."

Silence.

His anger at my unilateral decision coupled with his disbelief and confusion rendered him speechless and, for a moment, allowed me to stop trying to put a coherent thought together.

The next stoplight turned red, and Richard slowed the car to a halt. We sat motionless, both encased in our separate pain. I sighed loudly and withdrew to my corner, slouching closer to the car door. Each of us had taken a blow, and with this round over, we needed to rest for a moment and regroup.

The light turned green, signaling it was time to keep moving forward. I attempted again to explain what had seemed so clear and reasonable only an hour earlier. His jaw was set, and his eyes narrow. He showed all the signs of anger, but I sensed it was deeper than that.

I wondered what he was imagining. Could he be envisioning the same beautifully framed pictures of us I had envisioned, crashing to the ground and shattering? Pictures of the perfect ministry couple. Laboring together. Hand in hand changing the world. I knew these pictures needed to go or there would be no room for what God had for me. What I was less sure of at the moment was whether it had been necessary to break all that glass in the process. Perhaps I could have found a way to carefully open the frames and remove the pictures without causing so much damage. But all I could do now was try to keep from cutting myself on the shards.

And so began my rebel journey. A single no that forever changed my path. A messy, imperfect, beautiful no.

Into an Unknown Future

Fifteen years later I'm forced to acknowledge that, as defining moments go, this was not really earth shattering. More of a whimper than a battle cry, this scene, nonetheless, marked a line in the sand to which I've often returned as a reminder of both my strength and my weakness.

After a well-established history of living in "I should," I took a baby step toward "I desire." Though filled with shame for even having a desire, I stumbled forward into an unknown future. But how did I get here? Why all the drama and buildup for a single syllable word?

In hindsight, I had a history of stepping out in a different direction. I didn't always do what I perceived was expected of me, but I rarely defied an established authority—like the church or my husband—in the process. At least not to their face. My rebellion was stealth. I waited until no one was paying attention, then slid in the back door—smiling my good-girl smile all the way.

Some people call that passive aggressive. I called it survival. Allow me to share a brief history.

The Early Journey

My gait was brisk and intentional. I wanted to run, but even more, I wanted to avoid attracting attention. Relieved to spot an open pay phone, I pulled the phone card from my backpack and mouthed the numbers as I pressed them on the keypad. I was a sophomore in college, cell phones had yet to be introduced, and I needed to talk to my mom.

I can't remember if she answered. I do remember why I called.

A few months earlier, my parents had dropped me off in Tempe, Arizona, where I began school at Arizona State University (ASU). After growing up in a Christian family in a rural, church-saturated community, attending twelve years of Christian school, and one year of Christian college, I had decided it was time to leave the protective bubble that was my life. From what I could see, the world out there seemed expansive and opportunity rich.

In a final act of maternal involvement, my mother had connected me to a fellow transfer from Iowa whose parents she knew, making my official friend tally one in a sea of forty thousand students. The weekend before school started, I attended a party at her apartment with enough alcohol, drugs, and sex to put us in the running for the soon-to-be-popular *Girls Gone Wild* series. Far from tempted to participate, I felt the deep ache of regret as life outside the bubble quickly lost its iridescent shine.

My first class—Anatomy/Physiology—convened in Murdock Hall and boasted more students than my small-town high school. In the first week, my professor used the phrase "the apes from which we evolved," and I knew I was no longer in the proverbial Kansas (or Iowa). In Holistic Health, we engaged in lively discussions about auras, chakras, and, unexpectedly, abortion.

The phone call I made to my mom came after the abortion discussion.

In my class of thirty, I had been one of two students who stood up—literally—as being opposed to abortion. You'd think I'd remember the other stander, but I was too terrified to notice. There were questions I couldn't answer, reasons I couldn't articulate, and I knew I had just failed the test of living in the world. I wanted to go home.

I decided to stay, but my year was rocky. Every day on campus was an exercise in loneliness and self-hatred. So much for the rebel life.

While it was true that I had wanted to break out of my sheltered life, I picked ASU for a slightly less noble reason. During my year at a Christian college, I had begun exercising compulsively, and the warm temperatures of the desert southwest meant an outdoor track year round. I was just beginning to binge and purge, and I hoped a change of scenery would give me a fresh start. But not only were my old demons catching up to my move, new ones were meeting me there. My little experiment was quickly being derailed by depression and bulimia.

My path changed with a connection to a church community that loved me. I began a journey of emotional healing and spiritual transformation. I entered treatment for my eating disorder and worked my aftercare program diligently. I grew by leaps and bounds, and I was living in a freedom I had never before experienced.

Life After Addiction

It wasn't long before I was discipling other women and being invited into broader leadership roles. Out of that community, I also met my husband, Richard. He was one of my first friends and remained so through both the lows of my eating disorder and the long recovery. We could talk for hours. I was captivated by his humor, kindness, and generosity. I'd never met someone so authentic, articulate, or able to bring such freshness to God's Word. Deep friendship ultimately blossomed into a dating relationship, and we were engaged soon after.

Our wedding seemingly marked the beginning of a great ministry partnership. We were both strong leaders who loved God and whose gifts appeared to complement each other. When Richard began seminary, I was able to be the primary breadwinner. When a ministry position became open earlier than we anticipated, I was his right-hand woman.

I would sing, speak, disciple, counsel, plan retreats, lead small groups, strategize—all while working a full-time job.

Ministry was difficult on so many fronts. We were at a large church where every Sunday our worth was measured by how many people showed up at our meeting. Every event was a gauge of our leadership and spiritual effectiveness, and other churches were viewed as competition.

In spite of all of that, I believed in the local church. It's where I had come to find my life and had received a second chance. I'd left a life of addiction and emptiness, and I wanted others to find that freedom, too. I certainly didn't want to go back to where I'd come from, and I filled my spare time with church activities—Bible studies, leadership meetings, camps, weekend events, and overseas trips. All that left little time for relationships with people outside the church.

I had returned to the bubble and by this time, I just wanted to escape it all. I wanted Richard to graduate from seminary and get a job so I didn't have to work and I could stay home and have babies and be the perfect pastor's wife. I knew I wouldn't be happy with that either, but it was the only other thing I knew to do.

Eventually, I got pregnant, but even with his full-time pastoral role I had to keep working part time to make ends meet. I was devastated. Actually, furious. So angry, in fact, that I didn't recognize the gift God had given me in working until many years later.

In retrospect, it was one of God's kindest gifts. It was during this time that I ended up leading a colleague to Christ and we started leading weekly Bible studies with our coworkers and their friends. None had a prior relationship with Jesus.

We met in the evening, and in spite of God's obvious favor and presence, it was a weekly battle to attend. I had to disregard the unspoken working-mom code: There shall be no evening or weekend commitments as penance for the regular abandonment of offspring. But it was the best decision I ever made, and I'm still amazed that God let me experience it.

There were no radical conversions, but lives were changed. Least of which, mine. It was so far from perfect and so beautiful. I made my boss cry, I got in an argument with a Mormon, and I missed a glaringly obvious good-Samaritan moment. But I had someone ask me straight out,

"So how do you become a Christian?" and I was able to give an answer. She didn't want to be one; she just wanted to know what it took. And I was faithful to respond.

Moving from full time to part time took a surprising toll on my identity. I had pioneered a program allowing me to remain in management while working fewer hours, and I expected to experience relief and freedom. What I found was that I missed some of the perks and influence of my more profession-focused days.

But I did have the balanced life I was seeking. I was distributing mediocrity equally throughout my roles. Life as the mother of a newborn was more taxing than I had anticipated. I struggled on and off with depression, but I kept doing what was expected of me.

When our second child arrived, I stepped down from leadership at church but still attended most events and camps and overseas trips. In addition, I was starting to do more speaking with women's groups around the area.

But it was child number three that opened up the chasm. Surprisingly, taking all three kids on a college mission trip deep into Mexico with our conversion van pulling a pop-up trailer wasn't the final straw. Even the fact that I was nursing the youngest and potty training the middle child didn't put me over the edge. But the end was near.

A few months later, I sat in a friend's living room with seven other women, all of us sharing our stories. As I processed the pain and pace of the last ten years, the floodgates opened, and I realized I was done. With my body fighting exhaustion, my soul shriveling, and my emotions threatening mutiny, something needed to change.

The discussion moved to solutions, and I felt an enormous burden lifting. I was free and light and joyful. Feeling so good, in fact, that I didn't want to wait a minute to get started. I had to tell Richard immediately so I could embark on my new path.

Deep down I knew my announcement would be met with a bit of resistance. But I had no idea how complicated it would be to unwind my ministry from my marriage, how controversial my decisions would soon become, or how time-consuming and difficult a new way of doing life would prove to be.

CHAPTER 2

The First Test

For most of my dating life, breaking up was more of a process than an event. I started with hints about my dissatisfaction, hoping my hapless beau would catch on and initiate a preemptive end to the relationship. If that didn't work (and it never did—not even once), I tilled the breakup soil with the revelation of some major emotional issue I was experiencing. This paved the way for the it's-not-you-it's-me talk, designed to convince him it was better for him that we not be together.

Even then, I rarely went cold turkey. I'd suggest more time apart, panic when he seemed fine without me, decide to try it again, remember why I wanted to end it in the first place, and ultimately become increasingly distant until the final conversation was just a formality.

Such was my breakup routine from a life of "I should."

Though I had been ineffectively hinting at my discontent for some time, the conversation with my husband in the car was an attempt to use my well-established emotional issues as a reason for my needed rest. This laid the foundation for next steps, but the journey was not over. It was just beginning.

The New Space

From that first conversation, I had asserted that lightening my load would bring more energy and freedom. But as the dust cleared, I found myself lost and alone in the open space. Far from free, I felt restless and ashamed.

What had I done? On the one hand I was ravenous for more rest, more alone time, more nothingness. I wanted time to pursue the path past "I should." On the other hand, without constant busyness (and therefore purpose) as my companion, I was floundering. I expected the act of saying no would produce immediate fruit, but I was as unhappy as ever. And now I had more time to consider my discontent.

Some days I doubted anyone had the kind of intimacy with God that they claimed. Other days I feared everyone had a better relationship with God than I and they'd soon discover my charade.

I was slowly sinking. And then, inexplicably, God intervened with a whisper.

At a gathering in her home, a wise friend read a section from Jan Johnson's book, *Enjoying the Presence of God* (NavPress, 1996). One sentence was all I needed. Jan realized, "I didn't need a great quiet time, I needed a God-centered lifetime."

Even now, as I recall this moment, I am undone. God's grace and kindness in revealing a new way was not in response to a request I had made. It was not the natural next step in a process of intentional spiritual maturing. I was out of ideas. I had no plan. I was a slave to my own hypocrisy and was too tired and stubborn to call out for help. I assumed this would be my existence, and I was resigned to a life of ineffective striving. I expected very little from God.

Yet he pursued me. Not confined by the small box in which I had placed him or limited by my lack of faith, he showed up to lead me on a journey I didn't know was possible.

I quickly realized I had grown tired of hearing myself talk in prayer and of putting words in God's mouth during Bible reading. I'd been analyzing and taking apart Scripture and was completely missing out on the enjoyment of God. I didn't know what it meant to have a "God-centered lifetime," but I knew it was what I wanted. I also knew my time with God was not helping me achieve it. So I quit. At least I quit practicing a discipline that was no longer moving me in the direction of God and love and freedom.

I began to get up every morning and simply sit with Jesus. I didn't read the Bible, and I didn't pray in the way I had in the past. I sat in silence, figuratively at the feet of Jesus, and waited. It had never occurred to me before that I didn't have to say anything during these times. But when I shut up, he suddenly seemed very near.

At the time, I didn't know there were hundreds of saints who had pursued God this way; that the history of the church had produced volume upon volume of practices that could guide me. But for the first time in a long while, I began to look forward to spending time with God each day.

And it was during these times that he began to show me a way forward.

Obedience Training

In the same way I had been reluctant to completely break up with my boyfriends, I was reticent to break off all ties to my former commitments. Any time I felt a burst of energy or a surge of shame, I was tempted to jump back into the things I felt I should do. Some days I couldn't remember why I had stepped out in the first place, and then I'd attend a meeting and be instantly thrown back into exhaustion and irritability. It was a toxic pattern for everyone involved.

As I sought counsel from others around me and sat and listened to God, a few truths emerged. Cutting out my ministry commitments had not solved all my problems, but it had created space for more insight. This new space, however, was uncomfortable, and I was in danger of simply filling up my life with new distractions. If good was to come out of the work I'd done, I needed to attend to my soul, or soon all this work would be lost in burnout.

So I sat. As I listened, a seed of a thought began forming. I sensed a nudge to say no to any new commitment or opportunity for the rest of the year. I had recently heard that when I had an idea that couldn't have been hatched by my brain, it was likely from God. This thought was definitely outside my ability to conjure up, but it made so much sense.

My vacillating emotions, conflicted motives, and lingering exhaustion made my decision making erratic and random. A game of pin the tail on the donkey would've produced more informed responses to requests I received.

And I needed practice saying no. It stood to reason that a season of repeated use would strengthen this much atrophied muscle.

Over the next weeks, the parameters of my experiment took shape. I didn't write them down or formalize them. They morphed out of experience as I continued to step forward on this new path.

In reality these parameters were more like daily affirmations than a set of rules. They were the truths I told myself (or mumbled under my breath) when the compulsion to comply welled up in my throat and I found myself wanting to plead, "Please don't hate me!" to ease the tension of my refusal. I resolved to say no without hesitation to any new commitment or opportunity for the remainder of the year. I promised myself I would not make excuses. "I am not taking on any new commitments right now," was a sufficient answer. And in a bold move, I determined I would not apologize for saying no.

The First Test

I recognized the number on my caller ID as being from the church where my husband, Richard, was a pastor. Maybe he was calling to tell me how wonderful I was. More likely he was trying to get a read on which Kelli would be greeting him upon his arrival home. Cheery Kelli? Frustrated-with-the-children Kelli? Teary Kelli? It really was a crapshoot these days.

"Hello?" I answered.

"Hello, Mrs. Gotthardt?" This was definitely not Richard, and his prospects for enjoying dinner with a happy wife were fading quickly. I knew this tone. Someone from church wanted something from me.

"Yes, this is Kelli." (I was trying not to be condescending, but seriously! Mrs. Gotthardt?)

"I'm calling from the children's ministry at church." I knew this day would come eventually.

The curse of the PK (pastor's kid) had struck, and one of my husband's offspring had said a swear word or bitten another child or, worse yet, told the Sunday school teacher that his mommy was sad a lot.

"Yes?" I said, bracing for what was next.

"Well." She sounded nervous with a touch of false optimism. It couldn't be good.

"I hope your kids are having a great experience in the nursery." Clearly she didn't understand the purpose of the nursery. The more appropriate question was, "Are you enjoying the two hours each week you feel like a contributing adult?" To which I would have responded with a hearty, "Yes!" But I was having a hard time getting a read on where this was going.

"We are asking all the moms of young children to volunteer for one Sunday a month in the nursery. If all of the moms participate, it probably won't even be that often, so can we count on you?"

As my heart rate increased and the familiar tightness in my chest rose up, I had a brief internal conversation with myself.

"But if not enough moms sign up, I'll be there every week!"

"Oh, I'm so selfish!"

"But I'm exhausted and it will take so much energy!"

"What will people say if I decline?"

"I'll figure out how to renege later. . . . I'll cry. I'll check into a mental institution so they'll know I'm in really bad shape, and then they'll feel awful for even asking."

"What would Jesus do?"

"Why aren't they asking all the dads?"

"Wait! I'm saying no to everything."

It was for just such occasions that I had made my say-no-to-everything rule. "I'm sorry. I'm not adding any new commitments right now." Although I hadn't managed to avoid apologizing, I was quite proud of myself for otherwise sticking to my script.

Long pause. She was obviously having an internal conversation as well.

"We're asking all the moms." Yep, I had already gotten that point, and I wasn't exactly sure how that helped, but I had clearly flustered her.

"I understand. I'm really not taking on any new commitments." If she could repeat herself, so could I.

"It's not every week and it's just that since you're a pastor's wife, it seems like you would understand and we were kind of counting on you."

Why would "they" count on me? She didn't even know me. She had called me Mrs. Gotthardt. She had no idea the fragile state I was currently in. Allowing me to care for small children could only demonstrate "their" clear lack of discernment.

But I digress.

"Yes, it makes sense, but I just can't do it right now." Quick note for those who didn't grow up in church. Adding the word *just* to any statement or prayer is somewhat like invoking the right of parley to a pirate (see *Pirates of the Caribbean* for the complete explanation). You cannot be harmed or criticized if you say *just* as in "I'm just trying to help you be more like Jesus" or "Lord, I just have this one, small request. . . ."

"Well, we're just asking this of all the moms who use the nursery." This was the big guns. A third repetition, the use of *just*, and a dose of guilt because I take advantage of this service. Well played.

"I'm sorry." And I really was by this point. "I'm going to have to say no."

It was over. The goal was to be able to say no without guilt, to things God was not asking me to do. Unfortunately, I had no idea what God was asking me to do at this point, so I felt flustered and anxious. And, while I was exceedingly glad not to be working in the nursery, I also felt tremendous guilt.

In another time, I would have been your go-to woman. Not because of my servant's heart, but because I hated to say no. So, I didn't.

I often said yes to events occurring simultaneously and rationalized that I'd figure it out later. Who does that? If I did summon the courage to say no, it was usually after an initial yes, a dramatic whining session with my husband, and a lengthy, spiritualized explanation (and possible white lie) for my deep regret in having to decline.

But this was a new day. I had acknowledged that I was broken and burned out. So broken I needed to completely reboot. Shut down the way I was currently operating, clean out all the programs I wasn't using, and then rebuild the system. Thus my revolutionary experiment—one year of saying no to any new commitment.

And in other pride-crushing news, my exodus from Richard's ministry had resulted in a huge growth spurt for the ministry in both numbers and spiritual vitality. Apparently, I was not the glue that had held it all together.

I was struggling to find my identity, and my feelings of insecurity contributed to a general malaise that I feared would continue to grow if left unattended. Appearing happy and "spiritual" was requiring more energy than before, and while my internal struggles were not currently apparent to the outside world, I wasn't sure how long I could keep up this delicate dance.

As the weeks wore on, the distressed reality of my good-girl unhealthiness began appearing beneath my optimistic, helpful exterior. Like the wallpaper peeling in my firstborn's bedroom, I feared the large chunks of my identity being torn off might expose ugly paint, not the priceless treasure I longed for.

But I was no longer a victim of what I perceived others wanted from me. I had choices, and I was certain that beginning to define my own journey with God would be the start of a new, energized era for me. Thus my exit from ministry responsibilities.

Saying no to new commitments was saying no to finding my worth in pleasing people or doing good things, and no to experiencing numbing unhappiness through activity. But more importantly, saying no was saying yes to finding new spiritual practices that would lead me to God. It was saying yes to continued emotional work and to physical habits that might lead to healthier brain chemistry and increased clarity for the path on which God was leading me.

I had no Plan B. I was counting on this to work, and I had just passed my first test.

CHAPTER 3

Backlash

As time passed, I fancied myself a role model for overworked Christians everywhere. Or at least Christians on my little island. Each rejected request brought with it a few new admirers. I never would have guessed moving forward with this plan of no might actually help me gain more approval and affirmation. I should have done this much earlier!

I was just beginning to enjoy my new folk-hero status when reality hit.

Yes, I had fans, but I also had detractors. And they weren't just overly pious rule followers. These were godly men and women, many of them friends, who felt uneasy about my actions. Wasn't I being a bit selfish? Might I not be a bad example for others who really should serve? I was a spiritual leader—like it or not—and people were watching. Perhaps I need not proclaim to everyone that I "quit my quiet time."

And of course the people to whom I was saying no were not big fans. When I said no to friends, the shame felt particularly heavy.

This all came to a head one Sunday morning when a good friend made a casual request as she sat next to me in church. She and her husband were planning an out-of-town trip, and she wondered if Richard and I would watch their kids for the weekend. She knew I was on a rampage of declinations, but I'm sure she figured our friendship and the circumstances would merit an exception.

To be fair, my original parameters were primarily centered around ministry and community obligations, so this may have been a gray area. But there was no stopping me now. Particularly for requests that were not only tiring, but instantly anxiety inducing. I'm not a kid person. I love my own children, and I sometimes enjoy other people's offspring in small doses. But the chaos of adding three active children to my three active children for an entire weekend felt daunting. Bedtime alone would have put me over the edge.

So I said no. Didn't even hesitate, as I recall.

It's time I pause for reflection. As I write this, I'm more than a decade down the road from this incident. I know taking time to establish boundaries and regain my equilibrium was crucial to my spiritual, emotional, and physical health. I know I eventually was able to say yes to things that were uncomfortable, and I do wish I was writing a book that highlighted my sacrificial life. Yet saying no was a necessary part of my journey because I am a wounded and selfish person who needed to make some changes. Still, it's just not that inspiring. It feels quite sacrilegious to celebrate not helping people. Even in an airplane emergency, you don't root for the mom who puts her mask on first until she's successfully saved her child. I was not yet to the child-saving part of the story, so on some days it felt like I was going to fumble with my mask until it was too late to help anyone.

Now, back to our story.

I said no. I sensed some disappointment, but I trusted they'd find someone else, and we'd move on.

The next week as I walked into church, my friend's husband approached me and directed me to follow him out to the lobby so we could talk. The request from a week ago was long gone from my consciousness, and I surmised he might be planning a surprise for my husband that he wanted me to be a part of. I followed him to a quiet place and turned to face him. I smiled as I inquired about what he wanted to say. He was resolute, though slightly uncomfortable, as he began to speak.

"I heard you were unwilling to watch our kids while we get away next month." He paused as if to give me an opportunity to defend myself or perhaps retract my earlier decision. I did neither. I nodded yes as I looked at him quizzically.

"Frankly, we're really surprised at your response. And disappointed. We're not sure how your response reflects godly character. When you're a part of a community, you should be willing to help other people out. We all do things that we don't want to do or that tire us out. But this is not how the body of Christ operates."

My insides were spinning. I focused on breathing and not crying. I had lost all perspective. Shame enveloped me like a heavy fog, and my knees buckled under the pressure. Of course, what he said was true. In community you do things you don't want to do. You put the common good above your own desires. And my pendulum may have swung too far to the other side. There were no easy answers. But even Jesus sometimes walked to the next town, leaving people unhealed and uncared for.

He went on to inform me they had found another family to stay with their kids but he wanted me to know my actions had hurt them.

That's the problem with community—your actions affect other people. He had done the right thing in coming to me with his concerns. He valued community and knew unresolved hurt would eventually erode our friendship. I don't remember if I apologized or not—I hope I did. At the very least I hope I shared my gratitude for his honesty and willingness to have that difficult conversation.

Many years later I can see how setting boundaries helped strengthen me so that I could effectively participate in community later. But there are no guarantees and no formulas. It was my unhealthiness that brought me to this point in the first place and I would have to take responsibility for the hurt I might cause in the recovery process. This experiment was getting uncomfortably convicting and I wouldn't have recommended this path to any people-pleaser who hadn't received some sort of divine invitation.

The Other Side of No

The other difficulty with saying no became apparent when I desired to say yes. To make a commitment to say no in the midst of a bunch of bad options or burnout is one thing. But what about when you start to feel better and you get an invitation you'd like to accept?

Prior to this season of my life, I'd been speaking to some women's groups. This had been a dream of mine, but the stress of it was not worth the money. And I was a C-list speaker at best.

But just as I was beginning to get my bearings again, I received a phone call from a large women's ministry in the area. They wanted me to teach a number of breakouts at their next big event.

This was a conundrum.

I had passed up some neutral activities in this season, but I had not yet had an offer that represented something I longed for. If I said yes, I would be a hypocrite. A liar. Like the girl who tells each boy who courts her she's not interested in a relationship but then finds herself engaged to someone else six months later. Clearly she just wasn't interested in a relationship with *him*.

If this truly was God's idea—and I believed it was—then this was bringing up another issue. Trust. I feared that saying no to this event might be saying no to a future life as a speaker. What if this was my only shot? What if I was saying no to my destiny? Did I trust that if that was what God had for me he could make it happen even if I said no to this one engagement?

As I sat with the invitation for a while longer, I knew I could only respond in one way. I had to decline. I was testing God. I was learning that my activity had been largely based on my need to give myself every opportunity. I didn't want to miss anything, because at a heart level I believed that I had to make things happen. But that strategy had left me feeling depleted and useless. I was willing to try a different plan. What if I could learn to trust God for my future?

It sounds ridiculous and dramatic today, but when I phoned to say I couldn't speak at the event, I was relinquishing my dream to God. By then I knew God had much more work to do in me, and recovery from burnout was only the beginning.

CHAPTER 4

Be Still Some More

The jagged, red-orange formation split the rich blue sky in half. The contrast was stunning. I arranged my blanket on the grass underneath a large shade tree and settled in to this view for the morning.

The red rocks of Sedona are one of God's great cathedrals. Each time I visit, I find myself taken aback again at their majesty. They were the perfect setting for a day of silence and solitude. Each January the pastors' wives from our church headed up to this location to reflect on the previous year, enjoy time with God, and listen for direction for the next year.

That's what I was most excited for on this particular day. Instruction for the next year. I had successfully navigated a year of rest. Not just saying no to activity, but saying yes to more time with God. More intimacy. More love. More peace. In one of the great shocks of my life, it had worked! It wasn't without fallout, but for the first time in my life, I was tasting what I later came to describe as "spiritual formation." Change that only God can produce. I wasn't just acting differently—I was different.

And now I was ready to branch out. Ready to start doing more. Saying yes to activity. I salivated at the possibilities. What might God and I accomplish this year? With my growing godliness, open schedule, and renewed energy, I would be a spiritual force to be reckoned with. I began quieting myself before God. Eyes closed, intentionally slowing my breath so I could relax more fully. I sat in God's presence for a quarter of an hour without speaking. My thoughts occasionally turned to plans of my week ahead or an errand I needed to run, and my attention was sometimes diverted by a pesky bug or a chattering bird. But I always drew my thoughts back to my focus on being in God's presence. "I'm here, Lord," I would repeat when I found my thoughts wandering.

I pulled a Bible out of my bag and began reading from the Psalms. It was easy to praise today. My heart was full, and I sensed God's presence in the beauty found all around me. I moved on to a reading from the Gospels and was again reminded of the wonder of Jesus.

I had an agenda for the day, but I didn't want to get to it too quickly. I'm a fan of delayed gratification and a sucker for pomp and circumstance. I didn't find out the sex of my two sons before they were born because I longed for the emotion of the moment—the growing anticipation of a soon-to-be-revealed secret and the feeling I knew I'd experience when I heard the doctor say, "It's a boy!"

That's what I was expecting on this day. Later in the morning, God would be unveiling our plan for the year, and I didn't want to get to it too quickly. I would savor the buildup. I was setting the stage for a dramatic revelation.

I spent another hour prayerfully reviewing the previous year. Where had I seen God at work? Where had I missed him? Who had I hurt? How had God grown in me? What idols had he revealed? I was again reminded of the way God had intervened in my life over the last year. How he had shown up when I was at my end and given me a plan and a path and new life. How he had been faithful with his promises to me and had given me more than I had even known to ask for. It was a sweet period of remembering.

And then it was time. I closed my notebook and my Bible, and I sat. I heard the leaves rustle and faraway traffic, and I paused before I asked, "What will we do together this year?"

The sky was deep blue and the grass, bright green. The mountains now seemed shimmery gold with the sun's reflection. My lips were turned up at the corners, already formed in a quiet smile.

I waited.

I wasn't in a hurry. The stillness only heightened my anticipation and I settled into a rhythm of silent praise and patient waiting.

The thing about attempting to discern the voice of God is that it often borders on schizophrenia. Was that God, or did I just think that thought in my own brain? What's the difference? How can I tell? After a year of sitting quietly, I was beginning to more easily recognize God's voice. This type of discernment was a little-used muscle up to that point, so it took some practice. Of course, there were no guarantees—I could definitely be making it up. But I most often heard his voice in the pages of Scripture, and that's how I was beginning to recognize him. When random verses came to mind, I just went with it. And if I asked for direction from God and then a really crazy idea came to mind, I usually assumed it was from him. I was a pretty conventional woman, and my ideas were thoroughly practical and relatively safe. If a crazy solution popped into my head, I definitely sat with it for longer.

Like the time I stopped at the bikini car wash. It was a hot summer's day in Phoenix, and I was hurrying home from work. In the distance I noticed a spray of water, and as I approached, I observed a group of tan young women in tiny swimsuits parading around the sidewalk, advertising their new business—a bikini car wash. My first thought was, "Someone needs to call the city council and get rid of this eyesore." The line of cars waiting to be, er . . . serviced indicated this might not be the view of all citizens.

But more alarming than the various forms of undress, was my second thought: "I should get my car washed there." Even as I heard myself think it, I laughed audibly. It made no sense. But as I sped past the sunglassed men in the waiting cars, I found myself feeling compassion for these women, not disdain. That was new. And it was my first indication that this message might be something more than a heat-induced, delusional thought. God was giving me direction.

It was such a crazy idea I felt I should run it past a few other people. Like my husband. I didn't broach the topic as soon as I walked in the door after my commute. That wasn't the kind of thing you just blurt out. In fact, by the time I got home, I was already rethinking the whole this-is-from-God idea. We were attending an event at church that evening, and it wasn't until we were in the car, heading out for the night, that I mentioned what I'd seen. It was more a conversation filler than a request for insight. I described the scene as I drove by and the sadness of these women participating in their own objectification and the creepy men ogling them behind sunglasses and tinted windows. And then, as to not appear crazy, I qualified my next sentence with my fear. "I'm probably going crazy, but I had a brief thought that I should get my car washed there." See how I did that? I acknowledged the possibility, therefore dramatically lowering the chances that I really was crazy.

I waited for Richard to look at me with pity. To shake his head in disbelief at yet another one of my irrational ideas. To my surprise and joy, he thought it was brilliant, or at least really good. I'd initially determined that an affirming response from Richard would be a sure sign my idea was from God. Now I wondered if maybe I'd been a little hard on Richard. Perhaps I wasn't giving him enough credit, and I'd misjudged how he'd respond. So I put my idea to one more test. I decided that if I was going to do this crazy thing, I needed a female accomplice, and that would be the test of whether or not God wanted me to do this.

Once we arrived at our destination, I began looking around for a woman who might be up for this. I was only going to try this once. I needed to hear a strong yes from her if I was going to move forward. Entering the building, I saw a young woman who'd been a part of our lives for some time. She'd come to faith in Jesus within the last couple of years, and Richard had recently officiated her wedding ceremony. She might be up to join me, or she might not. But her answer was going to be my litmus test.

I approached her enthusiastically, and we exchanged greetings. I asked her to listen to my crazy idea. I began by telling her the story as I'd recounted it to Richard. Her eyes got wider and wider as I shared, and when I finished, she exclaimed, "You will not believe this!" Chances were I would, but I was game to play along.

She went on to describe her lunch break that afternoon. She worked downtown and had left her building to grab something from one of the numerous food stands in the area when she came upon one she'd not seen before. A bikini hot dog stand.

The odds of that happening were definitely greater in Phoenix than in most other metropolises in the country, but still. Her response had been similar to mine, and she was thrilled to accompany me to the bikini car wash. Nothing miraculous or out of the ordinary happened on that day. In fact, it was quite awkward. But God was teaching me to follow him and not worry about outcomes. This had been his idea, and I was learning to hear his voice.

Saying no had been one of those crazy ideas I would not have processed on my own, and it had turned out quite well. I was developing some confidence in the promptings of the Holy Spirit, and I was willing to give just about anything a try.

Back in Sedona, I took a deep breath, desperately trying to soak it all in. I prepared myself to hear from God again. As I exhaled, he broke the silence.

"Be still."

I wasn't sure how much stiller I could be, but perhaps God was preparing me to wait for a bit more. To not expect his answer right away.

I pushed the hair out of my eyes and resumed my quietness. "Be still," he said again.

I felt like he was talking a lot for someone who was asking me to quiet down. And then it hit me. He's not talking about now. He's answering my question. If I'm hearing this right, God is telling me that the thing we're going to do together next year is be still.

That can't be right. Then I began to argue.

"Lord, how can this be? I'm going to get bored. No one's going to understand. I promised it would just be for a year." And then the final blow. "How can I glorify you while I do nothing?" Tears were forming at the corners of my eyes as I lifted my head to gaze blankly into the open sky. In front of me the red rocks towered.

"Kelli. What is the mountain doing?" I heard him say.

"Nothing," I replied.

"That's right. Nothing. It is still, and it causes you to praise me."

I'm no expert on hearing from God. That little conversation may sound like heresy or just plain silliness, but I assure you, I could not have gotten to that conclusion on my own. It wasn't an audible voice. But as sure as the rather large nose on my face, God lovingly rebuked me in that moment.

There was nothing left to say. I was exhausted. God had answered my prayer, and his response was not what I had expected. It was still early in the day, and there was plenty of time to set about surrendering myself to his plan—being still some more.

Unfortunately, that is not what I did.

CHAPTER 5

Life in the Third Row

At church camp one pubescent summer, we female campers got the awkward (or awesome—depending on how good you looked in a leotard) opportunity to partake in a new fad called Jazzercise. This was prior to Jane Fonda or the dominance of aerobics in gyms across the country. Heaven only knows how our little Midwestern enclave managed to be on the cutting edge of culture. Someone on the planning committee must have been from the big city.

This was a bit of a coup. Secular music was playing, and we were moving our bodies to it. It sounded suspiciously like dancing—which was strictly forbidden in our church tradition. The closest we'd gotten to dancing prior to this move was acting out the motions to "This Little Light of Mine." This had potential. I was still years away from my groundbreaking article in the school newspaper on why we should have a prom instead of a banquet (creatively titled something along the lines of "Footloose for Real"), but I did enjoy pushing the envelope.

I was also frighteningly adept at reading a crowd. My superpower was quickly assessing the way the social winds were blowing, and I sensed some of the girls thought the whole thing was stupid. Ipso facto: I should probably think it was stupid, too.

Internally, I loved it. I loved the exercise, the dancing, and Barry Manilow's pure voice as he belted out "Mandy." Not to mention I was pretty good. But externally I put on a different face. I worked hard to make it look like it was easy while exhibiting disinterest and aloofness.

It seemed I was going to have my cake and eat it, too. Until the teacher inadvertently thwarted my plan.

On the second-to-last day of camp, our Jazzercise instructor advised us that some of the girls would get to perform the routine we'd been working on in front of the parents at the final talent show. She explained that if we wanted to be considered for that exhibition group, we needed to stand in the front two rows during that day's rehearsal. She would be choosing the final group from within those rows.

This was going to be a challenge for me.

On one hand, I was an achiever. If there was an award to be won, I wanted to possess it. I wanted (needed) to prove I was good enough to make the cut. On the other hand, to put myself in the front two rows would expose my desire and set me up for potential ridicule from my peers. My heart and mind were racing. I wanted to be chosen, but I didn't want to be exposed as wanting to want to be chosen. As the rows started forming, I looked around at what everyone else was doing. In a moment of cowardice I set myself up in the third row. But not without a plan.

As the music started and the girls began to move, just like I'd anticipated, the rows got a little messy. As I gracefully executed another grapevine step, I made sure to blur the line between the second and third rows. With each subsequent move, I remained uncommitted to a row. This was an omen of my future.

The music stopped, and the class ended. Our instructor advised that she would be informing the chosen girls later in the day. I felt pretty proud of myself and was dying to know if my evil plan had been a success. Here's how I hoped it might work. The instructor would approach me and tell me I'd made it. I would later explain to my friends that there had been some sort of mistake, but I felt bad so I had to say yes.

You can imagine my feeling of triumph as I saw the instructor walking toward me a few minutes later. Unfortunately, things didn't go exactly as I planned. Evil plans are so difficult to control. I was standing with a peer who had been very vocal about her disdain for the whole thing. Looking back, that makes sense because she didn't have a love of physical activity or any coordination to speak of. I don't know how

I missed that motivation at the time, but I barely understood my own motives, let alone the motives of others.

Instead of announcing that I had been chosen, the instructor asked what row I had been in. "I couldn't tell if you were in the second or third row." I knew she wouldn't be asking me this if she weren't prepared to offer me a spot on the prestigious camp dance line, but I also knew I was going to be required to commit to a row in front of everyone. This was not how I'd planned it. My uncoordinated friend glared at me. "You were in the third row." Just like that the decision was made for me. And it was addictively satisfying. I had managed to prove that I was good enough to be chosen without making a commitment or compromising my image. What a dangerous precedent.

Twenty years later, I was still playing that same game.

A New Obedience

After encountering God that day in Sedona, I moved on with life. I left that weekend still pondering the meaning of the instruction I had been given. Not that God had been cryptic, but I wasn't ready to commit to another year of stillness. So I determined to remain unresponsive and noncommittal—dancing between the rows.

Without noticing the subtle shift, I stopped seeking God. I was no longer in burnout, and I felt self-sufficient. I didn't have as deep a need for the rest that God had provided a year earlier, so I moved ahead on my own. In my mind, I wasn't choosing to disobey, but I wasn't exactly choosing to follow, either.

I was getting more opportunities in both ministry and business. I was working as a consultant and the jobs were coming in. By late February, on top of my role as mother of three young kids, wife of a pastor, and the newly blurred lines of my activities in ministry, I had a longer-term client.

In the midst of this I was given a do-over on my Jazzercise failure. An opportunity presented itself for which I knew I should position myself squarely in the third row. But it was a big deal. It was a position working for someone who had a "name," and I wanted to prove I could do it. After being presented the opportunity, I sat down with Richard and outlined the options in front of me. He was not a fan of me taking the job. It would involve a lot of work, travel, and pressure. It also had a high possibility of never getting off the ground. I knew he was right, but I wanted it so badly.

Without formally committing to do the job, I kept attending the meetings and discussing the project. I expressed my concerns and shared my packed schedule but continued to hang around. I committed to one small thing, then another, and then another.

Suddenly I was heading the project, slowly sinking into depression, and wondering what had happened.

Breakdown

My breakdowns often occur while driving. Maybe that's because after I drop my kids off at school, it's one of the rare spaces where I'm alone. Or maybe it's because, for a rather large chunk of my life, I was the official chauffer for three small humans. Regardless, this breakdown had been coming for a number of months. Life had steadily picked up speed, and my energy levels had waned in direct correlation. I wanted to throw up my hands in exasperation, claiming ignorance—"I don't know what happened!"—but the truth was I knew exactly what had happened.

I knew too many people in this square mile (which included my home, my church, and my kids' school) to fall apart like this in public. Even within the protective shell of my car, I felt exposed. But the sobs wouldn't stop. I had exactly one-quarter mile to pull it together before I arrived at school to pick up my kids. For those last moments, I just wanted to surrender to the catharsis of tears.

That day marked a dramatic ending and a new beginning. It was mostly dramatic in my head, but the past year had been so punctuated with aha moments it was difficult to calibrate my emotional gauges. Once again I found myself saying no in a highly charged environment. And like before, that two-letter word signified volumes of new knowledge and at least as many questions about the nature of God and his desires for me.

I did not realize that following Jesus involved more than adherence to the direct instructions of Scripture. I knew not to murder. I knew not to covet. I knew to pray, and I knew to make disciples. These were all clear directions. But since no one really explained the rules of listening to God, I did not realize that I was just as responsible to follow personal direction from God.

This concept is tricky because "hearing from God" has produced some wacky suggestions. Pleas for money, rationalization for sin, cults . . . just to name a few. But without going into the theology of this, I was quite sure God had clearly told me to be still. It jived with Scripture, others I shared it with had affirmed that it sounded like God, and even if I was wrong, it wouldn't cause me harm.

But somehow in not following this directive, I didn't feel like I was being rebellious. Unwise, perhaps—even careless. But certainly not rebellious. Until I felt trapped.

Earlier in the day I had visited a wise friend and poured out my soul. She was gracious and tactful. I wanted someone to tell me what to do, but she listened without judgment and asked questions instead of offering solutions. This was the gift she gave me—space for the Holy Spirit to work. My predicament must have seemed so simple for an outsider to spot. Particularly to someone who had been present when God gave me his directive. But she spoke nothing but words of healing.

I tried to focus as she spoke, but something was welling up inside me. My brain felt cloudy and dark, as if someone was dusting in there, making the air suddenly hazy and toxic. As my friend shared, her words stopped registering, and I felt my mouth open to speak. From deep inside me, seeming to bypass the cognitive process, the words were on my lips, and I pronounced my own healing, "I have to resign from the Timothy job."

Those words in themselves were not particularly surprising. I had declared the end to many a job in the privacy of a living room in the past. I would do it again in the future. But this was different. I hadn't planned those words. I didn't know they existed within me. But emerging from the confusion in my mind, I had suddenly seen clearly the path I had taken: the direct words from God in response to my inquiry, and my passive, but intentional response—"Thanks for the suggestion, but I'm going a different direction." And as I opened myself up to the gaze of Jesus, the words were almost involuntary.

My confidante continued with her train of thought until she too recognized the holiness of the moment. "I don't know where that came from!" I exclaimed, confused. Even more unsettling was my physical sensation—like a cork had just been popped and months of bottled-up anxiety and questions had been freed, leaving my soul feeling spacious and light. The brain fog of moments earlier was gone. My thoughts were clear and decisive.

"This won't be easy," I acknowledged. "But I know what I'm going to do." I went on to orally process what was occurring in my mind. By the time I left the comfort of that living room, I didn't recognize the woman who had walked in. I was reminded of the before and after pictures I had taken when I had entered, then graduated from treatment for my eating disorder. My face told a different story after experiencing healing. That was also what happened in my friend's living room. I breathed deeply as I drove away and headed to pick up the kids from school. I wanted to remember that feeling. I wanted to remember the contrasts of those few hours. What disobedience—even passive disobedience—does to the body. And the fullness of restoration that comes with forgiveness.

I laughed out loud. Then I cried. Deep, heavy sobs of both remorse and joy. But mostly joy. Then I dried my tears, pulled myself together, and drove into the school parking lot.

What a gift to fully commit to the third row. Not because I had succumbed to peer pressure or because the competition was bad, but because on that particular day, I didn't need to prove myself. I was enough, and learning to dance was all the reward I desired.

Letting Go

Lord, I am willing to receive what you give,
release what you take, lack what you withhold,
do what you require, and be who you desire.
—ADELE AHLBERG CALHOUN,
SPIRITUAL DISCIPLINES HANDBOOK

Let us throw off everything that hinders and
the sin that so easily entangles.
—HEBREWS 12:1

CHAPTER 6

Letting Go of Having It All Together

I'm an overachiever. Even when it comes to mental illness.

Affectionately termed a "high functioning depressive," I am usually able to keep it together in public, even when clinically depressed. That's not to say everything is business as usual. Far from it. I have a hard time getting out of bed. I'm more irritable than usual, less creative, and people generally annoy me. I don't return voice mail, e-mail, or texts. And while I'm working hard to keep it together for friends and strangers alike, my family gets the brunt of my dysfunction.

My first bout of real depression hit in year one of our marriage. It was a subtle shift into a dark new reality that I was unequipped to navigate with any sort of intentionality. I assumed it was part of growing up. I was finishing college and working part time. Richard was working a night job. We had no money and no friends who were married. We were still interns in the college ministry at our church, and that took every spare moment. The reality of marriage felt suspiciously like dating except I couldn't get away when I needed some space.

No one labeled my condition as "depression," and I wouldn't have known what it was if they had. Prozac was just entering the market and was still under the radar in most church circles. I was an avid journal writer and filled notebooks with my hopeless self-talk. At times the cloud would lift for short periods, but it always returned. I accepted it as the way my life would be. I was only two years into my eating disorder recovery, so I was still involved in recovery groups and counseling. Even with my rapid emotional growth and healing, I mostly felt tired and sad.

Then the final plank of security was pulled out from under me. The college pastor we were working for moved away. This set in motion a series of events that, like Dorothy's twister, picked up my life and set me down in an even darker forest than before. Just months away from moving up to the "Young Marrieds" class at church and finally graduating from college ministry, Richard was told he could be the college pastor. It was his if he wanted it. It wasn't really a job offer per se, but more of a decision by default. After a couple of months of searching, they had not been able to find a good replacement. He had just entered seminary, and I was working full time, so this seemed a great scenario, even an answer to prayer. Although I never recall praying that prayer, vocational ministry was in our future, so earlier is probably better, right?

He was technically called "Assistant College Pastor" even though he wasn't assisting anyone. Never mind that he had little training and was a peer to many of the students in attendance. Most of them decided this was a good time to find another ministry, and soon this once thriving group was less than a third of its earlier size. At least now we were both depressed.

Decades later, we not-so-affectionately call this period "The Early Years." We say it with a look on our face like the dog just farted. Yes, it was that noxious. To me, these were the years when people left me. They just kept going away no matter how hard I worked to woo them.

Mixed in with the personal abandonment were a series of moral failures by other pastors on staff that damaged families, wrecked the faith of many, and left a trail of disillusioned souls struggling to recover. Depression seemed a reasonable response.

I had married a perseverer. So we persevered. We kept going, and I kept dreaming of the day we would leave. But we stayed and picked up the pieces when not one, but two pastors flamed out of ministry in the space of a week. We kept moving forward as men were hired around us, then released. We created stability when beloved staff members went on to bigger and better things. We weathered friends who recruited leaders out of our ministry, and the continued decline of the church overall. But as Richard began to hit his stride, these things mattered less.

The ministry had reached a tipping point, and God's Spirit was present. Two miles from one of the largest college campuses in the nation, we were seeing students come to Christ and be discipled. We were getting them connected in community and sending them all over the world to experience God in new ways. They were full of passion for God and were finding healing from broken families and past scars. We had a strong team of lay leaders whom we were equipping and mentoring.

With time and a fair amount of counseling, my early marriage was relatively happy.

After the birth of our third child, however, I began to experience a sense of extreme fatigue. I had been born with a congenital heart defect that I hadn't had evaluated in a while so I went to my doctor for a checkup. When I described my symptoms, he gave me a test. A written test. It was a test for depression, and I passed with flying colors (at least that's how I chose to see it).

Someone had identified my malaise, and apparently there were solutions to the faulty wiring in my brain. But this was not an easy call.

I left my doctor's office with a prescription and a week's supply of samples. But that didn't mean I had to take them. The argument in my head was making me dizzy.

Broken self: "If you were counseling someone else, you would tell them to take the medication."

Pious self: "This is a spiritual issue. Pills won't solve that!"

Broken self: "You're irritable with your husband and your kids. If there's a chance this could help, you should try."

Pious self: "This is surely due to your lack of discipline. If you would just work a little harder, I'm sure you could muster up some happiness."

In the end, I took the pills. Within a couple of weeks, I felt normal. I smiled easily. I didn't feel weepy or crabby or hopeless. I felt like Kelli. Gratitude mixed with guilt.

Around this time I started my own consulting business, and my ability to keep my emotions in a normal range was key to my success. I found myself thriving in this environment, adapting to new clients, meeting new people, solving problems, and making friends. With all that going for me, I must be doing something wrong. Taking an antidepressant seemed to be creating an unfair advantage for me. So I stopped taking it.

The deterioration was slow and subtle but did not go unnoticed by those closest to me.

By this time I had resigned from the Timothy job and was back on the road to listening to God and following more closely. If God said, "Be still," I would be still. So my continued battle with depression puzzled me. I was doing what God asked me to do so why was I still depressed?

Even more disturbing was the realization that my emotional health was affecting my spiritual health. My first strategy had been to attack my emotional issues with spiritual weapons. Pray more. Read more Scripture. Pray differently. I had to admit my strategy wasn't working as I continued to decline. It was somewhat like addressing a poor appetite by getting my teeth cleaned. The cleaning was necessary, but even when executed well, it was not helping my appetite. God's direction for me was to step back and address my depression. So I did.

Although I was quite convinced that brain chemistry was the primary culprit, I did find a good counselor to make sure I was covering all my bases. I was secretly hopeful that some deep wound hidden below the surface, once exposed, would rid me of all sadness and dysfunction and finally render me "normal." Alas, this was not to be, and even with more spiritual and emotional work, I could not dig myself out of my funk.

I did not want to go back on antidepressants. It was an inspirational mix of stubbornness, pride, fear, and laziness that drove me to that decision, but I was adamant. The one thing I hadn't tried was changing my diet and using natural supplements. It would require more work, but anything worthwhile was bound to have a cost.

Over the next month, I set to work changing my diet, exercising regularly, and ingesting over-the-counter supplements to help regulate my brain's chemistry. Progress was slow, but it seemed to be working. Small but noticeable changes took place in my behavior. At least from my point of view.

Looking back on this period, Richard and I have differing thoughts on the effectiveness of my natural strategy. In my memory, I'm smiling and skipping. In his, at least I'm not crying every day, and this is progress.

Ultimately, it wasn't enough. I couldn't keep the cloud away, and I eventually returned to a prescription. It felt like a personal blow. As I sat in the psychiatrist's office, I whined to him that I didn't want to be on an antidepressant. "No one wants to be on an antidepressant," he replied. Touché.

Months later I stood in front of three hundred women at a retreat in Colorado and shared the truth that I was broken. I asked them not to try to fix me. And I opened up about my little secret: "I need a pill to keep me functioning." I shared that I still felt shame about my need for it. My weakness in not being able to overcome this defect. But each night I thanked God for the gift of the medication that helped me connect meaningfully with God, my family, my calling, and my own heart.

I wondered if such a broken person had any right to stand in front of these women and teach them. Most of the women I'd heard speak at events like these shared only those areas in which they'd experienced mastery.

"I used to struggle with being depressed, but then I prayed and prayed and now I'm happy."

"I used to have low self-esteem, but then I correctly interpreted Scripture and it changed my life."

Wasn't that why they'd invited me to speak? Because I had something to offer that was better than what they were currently experiencing or what "the world" offered? If I couldn't even avoid depression, then wasn't all the spiritual wisdom I had suspect?

As the words were falling out of my mouth, I regretted my decision. I'd been cautioned more than once about over-sharing in a leadership role. I was pretty sure this qualified. I found myself subconsciously willing the women in the audience to keep liking me. To stop judging me. I smiled nervously as I spoke, hoping my quivering voice and awkward body language were not exposing my fear.

After my talk that night a number of women thanked me for sharing about my drugs. Each of them took antidepressants, and each of them felt shame. Apparently, they didn't need me to have it all together. My admission somehow moved them along a path toward less shame.

Somehow, it helped me, too.

CHAPTER 7

Letting Go of the Approval of Others

During this season of saying no and wriggling free of some unspoken tenets of Christian culture, I had an uncharacteristic weak moment. I was not a fan of "Christianizing" nonreligious activities. In my experience, this usually involved taking a fairly benign secular activity, sucking the fun out of it, then making it extra cheesy. So when my friend invited me to attend a Christian yoga class she'd discovered, I first had to suppress the urge to snicker. My friend was in her late sixties. Yoga was probably a good option for her. But her support and encouragement had proved critical to my journey, and this seemed a small sacrifice in exchange for life-changing wisdom.

I was not without my concerns, however. Not about the evils of yoga, but of looking foolish in public, which I believed was highly likely in any exercise labeled "Christian."

I bought a cheap yoga mat and arrived at the studio anticipating a high ridiculous factor. In my untried opinion, yoga was part dance, part stretching, and mostly fluff.

Running was real exercise. I was a runner. Yes, my chiropractor had recently informed me that I would be done running soon if I didn't increase my flexibility, but stretching was something you did after real exercise and preferably not in public with a room full of wannabe athletes who would feel superior to me because they could do the splits or coerce their foot behind their head.

As I perused the brochure while I waited for others to check in, I was surprised to discover there were different levels of yoga. Apparently there was a Power Yoga option. That had promise, but I soon discovered I would be participating in a "gentle" class. Sounding more like a laxative than a workout, I knew at least I'd be able to keep up. Although I believed the words *gentle* and *exercise* in the same sentence constituted an oxymoron, I signed the required waiver and found a place to unfold my mat on the floor.

I sat cross-legged on my mat and casually examined the room. Lit candles along the walls formed a soft glowing hedge. Natural sunlight from rectangular windows near the top of one wall provided the only other light, and I watched the dust dance in its rays like a natural fog machine.

Fifteen or so students surrounded me, but in this expansive dance studio the feel was open and spacious. The men and women in attendance were housed in a variety of body types and appeared to have a wide range of fitness. As an introvert I felt awkward and anxious in this room of strangers. I couldn't get a read on what I should be doing while I waited. Some were lying on their backs, others were engaged in various stretches, and still others sat chatting with their neighbors. I went with the stretching option.

Our instructor found her way to the front of the classroom and invited us to lie down on our mats and close our eyes. I suddenly feared I might leave this class in worse shape than when I arrived.

But as worship music filled the room and our instructor read Scripture over us and I started to relax—I mean really relax—for perhaps the first time in months, my attitude began to soften. Along with my heart.

Twenty minutes in we had finally reached the part where we stand up. "What's the rush?" I wanted to ask. "I was just getting started!"

I should have stayed in the prone position. Five minutes on my feet and I was gasping for air, my muscles were shaking, and my pride was crushed. All while wearing yoga pants. And to make matters worse, my sixty-year-old friend did not appear to be breaking a sweat.

Twenty-five minutes of up and down and inversions and warrior poses and I was begging for the mat. Finally it came, and we cooled down slowly until it was time for resting pose. This involved five minutes of worship music, Scripture, and prayer as I lay soaking it in. And tears. I had not expected the tears.

As I left the studio, I was both exhausted and exhilarated. I wanted more. Not just because yoga had proved to be actual exercise, but because my soul had been nourished in a way I'd not experienced in ages. I determined to continue a regular practice of yoga to help keep me spiritually, physically, and emotionally healthy.

Funny thing, looking back, is that at the time I believed I had lost a bit of my rebel edge by making this decision. I could see how some might be offended had I started attending yoga classes where there was a naked Buddha and Sanskrit chanting, but I feared this might make me look like a sellout. This was just the kind of thing I had been rejecting for the last couple of years.

As it turns out, this rebel act nearly took me over the edge.

Yoga Stresses Me Out

"Can I observe your class?"

Before me stood a harmless looking woman. She had long, straight hair, plain and unadorned on purpose. Dressed neatly without being showy, her demeanor was friendly and her posture, almost apologetic.

It seemed an innocent enough request. I was preparing to lead my weekly yoga class with teachers from my kids' Christian school and members of our church staff. After completing my yoga certification training six months earlier, I had started this after-school series as a ministry. The timing and location allowed teachers to come straight from their classrooms, unwind from the day, and get in some exercise before heading home for the evening. Because it was at the end of their work day, many church staff members and a few pastors (including my husband whom I'd coerced into attending) also took advantage of the class. About forty women and a few brave men participated in each class, and many expressed it was a highlight in their week.

After a year of regularly attending Christian yoga, I had been invited to attend the two-hundred-hour certification training to become a

Registered Christian Yoga Teacher. It was about time I put that exercise physiology degree to use. Through the process of certification, we spent hours studying the religious associations and origins of yoga and how Christian yoga was fundamentally different. I understood there were some who were concerned, but I naïvely believed that I could convince everyone that practicing Christian yoga was not dancing with the Devil.

I invited the observer to have a seat at the back of the room, and I walked to the front. This class was the same as every other. We began by lying on our backs while instrumental music played softly. It was a bright, soulful version of "It Is Well with My Soul." As the students began to relax, I read Scripture to them. I reminded them how deeply loved by God they were. I invited them to be present in the moment, leaving behind the stresses of the day and offering up the concerns of the evening. I encouraged them that in the stillness, the quiet, and the lack of activity, they were loved just because they were sons and daughters of God. Not for what they were accomplishing, but simply for who they were.

It's a beautiful thing to watch busy people begin to slow and open themselves up to the love of God. To watch shoulders relax and faces soften and an occasional tear slide down a cheek. To observe one's burden of performance lifted as he or she soaks in the smile of approval from their Abba, Father.

We moved through the next hour of melody and movement and ministry without incident, and afterward I packed up my mat and went home.

Apparently, so did my quiet observer. Only, she also packed up her children from the Christian school and took them somewhere else. The deal had been sealed when she saw me describe "Prayer Pose" (palms together, fingers point up). This dear woman had just heard a sermon about the evils of yoga and, particularly, "prayer pose." So that was it. No discussion, no questions, no words of anger. Just a single act designed to make a statement.

During the week, a few other families pulled their kids from the school in a move of solidarity. They no longer felt safe, and it was my fault.

I was troubled.

I had not been trying to make a point or flaunt my freedom. By that time I understood that not everyone felt comfortable practicing yoga. Earlier that year another woman who had been attending the class pulled me aside and shared that she had heard a Hindu woman speak about yoga and therefore no longer felt comfortable attending. I understood. She looked at me intently and asked, "Are you sure yoga is okay?" I could answer yes unequivocally. For me. God had shown me Matthew 7:15–20, so I told her to watch my life. "It is impossible for a bad tree to bear good fruit," I told her. "So watch my fruit." I insisted that she not violate her conscience to attend the class. We embraced and remained friends.

But now, not only did strangers who had never taken time to talk to me hate me; I had cost the school money and potentially started a battle in which I did not desire to engage. Other teachers and staff members assured me I had done nothing wrong, but the rumblings had begun, and soon the school board was involved.

Behind closed doors, I'm told, there were long discussions about "the weaker brother" and pagan customs. Churchgoers who'd admired me for years began avoiding me. My husband was stopped at church so people could give him a piece of their mind on the topic. Zealous adults even engaged my kids in debates about yoga. Staff members who had supported the class when it started, suddenly condemned it as foolish and irresponsible. Twenty years of good behavior out the window.

Being a rebel was getting really tough. Not only did I not think this was a rebellious act but I was actually a little embarrassed by my participation in such an overt evangelicalization of a secular activity.

Taking a Beating When I'm Down

I so much like to be liked. But this seemed a clear test straight from Jesus on how to live in the tension of being disliked. It also seemed impossible. I felt trapped. I knew what I was doing wasn't wrong. In fact, I believed I was actively engaged in life-giving ministry. But nothing I could say or do, no Bible verse I could quote or prayer I could say, would convince some people of this. To my recollection I had never been in this predicament—unsure if people approved of me. It was hard to tell because the condemnation came in the most unassuming packages.

One day a sweet elderly woman called and asked me to meet her to talk about how I got involved in yoga. By this time I was wearying of the conversation and appropriately gun-shy. But she sensed my hesitation and assured me she just wanted to hear my story. Hmm. Seemed harmless enough. I do like to talk about myself.

I arrived at church where we had decided to meet at the agreed-upon time. We exchanged pleasantries and walked over to an empty room where we sat facing each other on folding chairs. This was a rather large room and, unlike my first yoga experience, the empty space made me feel unprotected, not free. Just as she promised, she began by asking how I got involved in yoga.

And she listened—for at least the first three minutes.

I felt my story, while not gripping, was compelling enough to sit through. But I noticed very early on that she seemed distracted. So I summed up my happy tale, took a deep breath, and waited.

She began to speak.

I'm not sure what I expected, but I found myself taken aback by the force of her allegations. By the time she was finished, I had been accused of being duped by the Devil and blatantly leading others into idol worship. When I feebly attempted to defend myself by pointing to the enhanced spiritual lives of my students, she told me it was Satan disguising himself as light. There was no working with this woman. She folded her hands in her lap and paused. Her strident gaze seemed incongruent with her preschool-teacher intonation. "Do you know what the definition of yoga is in the dictionary?" I was pretty sure this was going to be on the test later, but I was also pretty sure I didn't want to know the answer.

"I don't," I replied regretfully.

"Well, let me read it to you." She no longer sounded like a sweet schoolteacher. Her hands shook slightly as she grabbed the folded piece of paper out of her Bible on which she'd written the definition. I had just registered the fact that she'd brought a Bible to our conversation. That should have been a red flag from the beginning.

"An Eastern religion . . ." She read the definition with the certainty of a chess master who'd just outsmarted her opponent. The hands that had so often been folded in prayer, trembled as she held the paper. She was convinced of the justice of her cause. She was defending Christianity and this church and everything good and right.

And then it was over. She'd stated her case, defended the faith, and held fast to her convictions. There was nothing I could say that would assuage her indignation. I let her accusations hang in the air. I let go of being right. I didn't try to appease her by telling her it was okay or that I agreed with her. I didn't try to coerce her into seeing things my way. No manipulative tears (although the tears were being held back by a very strained dam). Just a nod and a "Thank you for sharing your concerns."

I was shaken, but not destroyed. And, surprisingly, not particularly upset with this dear woman. Looking back now I feel a strange affection for her. She was not a combative person. It must have been difficult to muster up the courage to confront a perceived evil in her community. We had much in common.

I spent a few days considering whether it was wise to continue with the class. I had not signed up for this, but was it a message from God to stop or an invitation to a new way of being? In the end, I determined not to quit. And not just because I was stubborn. If I was going to follow Jesus wherever he led, discomfort and opposition—even from within the church—could not be the cause of a course change.

I was being shaped and molded by God. Learning to live without the approval of others while keeping my gaze focused on Jesus and my heart attuned to the Spirit. And even though I didn't recognize it at the time, I was learning to love people who disapproved of me. That may have been the greatest miracle.

CHAPTER 8

Letting Go of Being Nice

Nice is not a fruit of the Spirit. I wish someone had pointed this out to me earlier in my life. It might have saved me a lot of money on therapy.

I wasn't always concerned with being nice. When I was six years old I threatened to punch a neighbor boy in the stomach if he didn't quit teasing me. I said this while sitting on his porch on a humid, summer afternoon. He looked at me hard, wondering if I was serious. I was dead serious. Until his mother's voice drifted sweetly through the open screen door—"Good girls don't punch little boys in the stomach." She had a point.

But then, how was I to defend myself from boys who teased me? That's how I discovered niceness. I hid anger neatly away and turned on the charm. For many years I thought niceness had set me free. Until truth opened its mouth and began vomiting up all the ugliness I thought I had avoided. Literally. The first step in my rediscovery of anger was in treatment for my eating disorder at the age of twenty. But this has been no quick fix and I've moved forward in fits and starts.

Letting go of being nice has been the foundational task in my movement toward greater intimacy with God. As I opened myself to the discomfort of new emotions and untested responses, God continued to gently coax me toward freedom. These frightening and awkward experiences were the prequels to stepping down from all ministry responsibilities. Back before I knew I wasn't free I found myself in a thorny situation that required me to face my anger. And, then the revelation that anger wasn't even the bottom. Underneath it all was shame.

Anger and Shame

Mr. Williams was a force. Santa-like without the jolly. White hair, large belly, red cheeks, and a bellowing voice. Perhaps I'm being too hard on him. He laughed sometimes, but it frightened me.

He was my boss and my desk was right outside his office. I had no idea what he did in there all day, but I knew it was important because he had a title and an office and his own secretary.

I was a recent college graduate and still trying to figure out what I wanted to be when I grew up. I knew I didn't want this to be my future but those in authority seemed to like me, approaching me periodically with new opportunities. At the same time I struggled to grasp corporate culture. I didn't understand the idea of promotions or working up the corporate ladder. I was there to put my husband through seminary, then quit and have babies. I also lived to please. I didn't want to upset the apple cart or cause anyone to think poorly of me. Looking back, I was the dream lackey.

I was also naïve to a fault. In a therapy session years later, even my counselor was surprised by my complete lack of worldliness. This appeared in different settings. In one department meeting, Mr. Williams asked me if I could complete an extra assignment for him in a short period of time. Not understanding that this was (a) not really a request but an actual assignment, (b) an opportunity, and (c) a test, I quickly calculated my other work responsibilities, my obligations outside of work, and my fear of failure, and I honestly responded, "No, I don't think I have time for that."

The hush that followed was my first clue I might have broken protocol. I was instantly filled with shame. Not so much for politely declining the request of my superior, but for not knowing what I'd done wrong. Clearly there was a set of rules of which I was unaware.

And in that corporate conference room, I was transported to my childhood schoolyard. Shame. Then a resolve to never make this mistake again. Anger. Covered with niceness.

Childhood School Yard

My childhood school yard is much smaller than I remember. In my mind, the distance between the tetherball poles and the softball backstop is an expanse. More prairie than playground. But as the adult me surveys this oft-imagined field, I absorb the uncomfortable reality of trauma—left hidden, it magnifies.

I have a vivid memory of walking across the middle of this elementary school yard at night. Behind me, the harsh fluorescent glare of the gymnasium lights offered little lighting and no comfort. A few of my friends stood on the cement sidewalk outside the school, but they were more like little demons taunting me. "You slut!" they yelled. They paced and huffed and puffed. They were disgusted by me and full of rage at my bad behavior. I felt myself shrinking. Escaping inside myself; getting smaller and smaller.

In my memory of this event, I was frozen in the middle of the field. Terrified and alone. I didn't want to move so as not to draw any attention to myself, but my eyes darted back and forth, desperately searching for someone who would rescue me.

In reality, I kept walking forward. And not by myself. I was with a boy. I don't remember exactly which boy, but he was one of the limited options in my small, private-school dating pool.

About two hundred yards to my left was the bank of pine trees that bordered the school property. It was behind those trees where I had my first kiss a couple of years earlier in fifth grade. A sweet, innocent peck that was the culmination of what felt like hours of standing next to each other, trying to figure out how this was supposed to work. After all the awkwardness and pressure, I must not have found the experience to be worth it, because as we emerged from behind the trees together, I turned to him and summarized my feelings by announcing with a sigh, "I'm glad that's over. I'm never doing that again." His surprised look clued me in on the fact that I was supposed to like it. Mental note.

But those innocent days were gone. Two years later, things moved more quickly, and on this night I found myself heading to the back of the school yard toward the "fort." The fort was a big brown wooden play structure next to the softball backstop. It was made of logs and planks and had bridges and slides and ladders and plenty of places to sit privately with a boy, hidden from preoccupied adults inside the school and curious peers on the outside.

I wanted to run away, but where? I couldn't turn back. The demons were waiting on the sidewalk to condemn me. I feared they'd devour me if I so much as turned my head.

Step. Shame. Step. Shame. Step. Shame.

How did I not know that this move would be a disaster? I told myself I was such a fool. That this was all my fault. I deserved the accusations. I had told this boy I would follow him. I had made poor decisions, but I'd be strong and not make any more waves.

I would learn not to make this mistake again.

Back to the Boardroom

After the department meeting, a manager who had taken me under her wing reprimanded me. "You can't say no to Mr. Williams! Especially in front of his whole staff! What is wrong with you?" I was wondering the same thing.

After my initial faux pas, Mr. Williams warmed up to me. This was good news because I had quickly learned that in a fast-moving, start-up organization, if I was to accomplish what I'd been tasked with, I needed the favor of men like Mr. Williams.

Like all department heads, Mr. Williams occupied a rather large, rectangular office. His was an interior office so the only window and door were on the short wall that opened into his secretary's large cubicle. I sat directly to the right of his office. When he worked at his polished mahogany desk, he couldn't see me, but I never knew when he might appear at his doorway to survey his department. This motivated me to keep busy. Sometimes he would saunter out of his office and stretch, as if he'd been doing some serious work. Then he'd lean over the wall of my cubicle and make awkward small talk. This wasn't my favorite way to pass the time, but it was part of the job.

One day I heard him calling my name before he even got to his door. "Ms. Gotthardt, can you help me?" He lowered his voice a little as he exited his office and ambled over to my cubicle. "Can you sew on a button? Normally I'd ask Renee, but she's in a meeting." Renee was his secretary, and I'd never wished she was sitting at her desk more than at that moment.

Contrary to what my husband believed, I did know how to sew on a button. And while I wished Renee was there to complete this task, I'd already learned that the answer to any of Mr. Williams's requests was yes. In retrospect, a tiny little red flag was raised in the deep recesses of my gut, but what could be the harm? "Sure," I replied, careful not to show any hesitation.

He summoned me into his office and closed the door. Then closed the blinds. He handed me the button, needle, and thread, and reclined in his comfortable office chair. He pointed to the place on his shirt where the missing button belonged and invited me to commence sewing.

I hadn't thought this through, but I definitely had not expected him to still be in the shirt when I sewed on the button. Again I attempted to appear calm and nonchalant.

Shame.

I processed my stupidity internally. "Of course you want me to sew this button on your shirt while you're wearing it! I mean, I guess it would be weirder if you took the shirt off." I detached from the moment and proceeded to sew. I was so close to him! I could feel his hot breath, and I was doing everything in my power to avoid actually making contact with him or his undershirt.

I finished and walked out. He didn't get up from behind his desk. Renee had returned from her meeting and gave me a puzzled look as I exited his office.

"I was sewing on a button," I said without making eye contact. Why did I feel guilty?

She shook her head in disbelief. "How'd he convince you to do that?" She wasn't expecting an answer.

Over the next couple of weeks, Mr. Williams periodically called me into his office to fix his tie or reattach his suspenders or flatten his collar. I could feel myself shrinking. I began avoiding my cubicle in hopes I could escape his requests. I told no one. I didn't even acknowledge it to myself.

One morning I stopped at my desk to grab a few things before heading over to a different department. Mr. Williams was in his office, so I slid into my cubicle from the back hoping to avoid detection. Before I could gather my things and escape, I sensed him hovering over my cubicle.

"Well, well, well, Ms. Gotthardt," he taunted while shaking his head. He had a smile on his face, but it didn't feel friendly. I strained to stay focused and appear busy.

"I thought you were a good girl. But in the dream I had about you last night . . . (dramatic pause) . . . you were not a good girl at all."

Something snapped in me. I didn't speak, but I had to hold back an audible sob. I wasn't about to cry really, it was more of a scream and vomit. I smiled weakly and left.

I assumed something was wrong with me that I had reacted so strongly to this statement, but I needed to tell someone. And I only knew one person who felt safe. Jeannette.

On my first day at this company, I sat in New Hire Orientation listening to all the policies and procedures while signing agreements and waivers. In the middle of the day, a woman opened the door with enthusiasm and exclaimed, "Welcome!" I liked her instantly. The Human Resources person at the front of the room introduced our happy intruder as Jeannette and told us she was a trainer. I didn't know such a thing existed, but at that moment I hoped I could someday become a trainer like this woman.

By the time these events took place, I occupied the position Jeannette had held when I met her on that first day. We had much in common, and I loved her humor, her care for her staff, her authenticity, and her strength. I trusted her, and I knew she cared about me.

As I walked into Jeannette's department, I began to doubt myself. "I'm such a freak! I'm making a big deal out of nothing. I'm just going to feel like an idiot when I tell her what he said." Somehow I kept walking, and I peeked my head into her office.

She looked up and smiled.

"Got a minute?" I asked.

"Sure. Sit down. What's up?"

I closed the door behind me so others wouldn't overhear. I feared they would think I was overreacting.

"Bob just told me he had a sexual dream about me last night," I reported as if I was totally cool with it and thought it was kind of funny. Although we were required to use formal titles when addressing department heads to their face, we definitely called them by their first names in private. Jeannette invited me to give some more details, and soon I was not only recounting the day's dream comment, but also the missing button and the other incidents.

Jeannette's next words saved me that day. "You're kidding me! That perverted little twit! You go back to Bob and tell him that scenario will *only* happen in his dreams. Then come back here and hang out with us for the rest of the day!"

In another year or so there would be processes in place that would have allowed me to file a complaint with Human Resources. I would have walked quietly to the HR representative and calmly recounted my experience. I would have been required to write up a formal report, and she or he would have sat and listened to me with detached sympathy, careful to appear caring without making any judgments. Who knows, Mr. Williams might have undergone some disciplinary action given his behavior with other women.

But on this day I needed to speak it myself.

I was so energized by the realization that I wasn't crazy that I marched back to my cubicle ready to say my line. I had no idea how I would move the conversation around to a place where it was appropriate again, but I didn't care. I felt strong.

I shouldn't have worried. Clearly, Mr. Williams wasn't ready to let it go. As soon as he saw me approaching, he emerged from his office with a smirk on his face. He handed Renee a file and muttered my name under his breath. "Kelli, Kelli, Kelli." I couldn't believe it was happening. He turned to look at me and as he walked back into his office he sighed, "Not such a good girl."

I could feel the blood draining from my face as I braced myself for what was coming. All my life I'd been pretending to feel confident, and it was finally paying off.

I laughed, like I found the comment amusing. I planted myself in the doorway to his office and glared at him. "Bob, you wish! That will *only* happen in your dreams."

My voice was trembling as the surge of adrenaline pulsed through me like an electric shock.

I turned and walked away so I wouldn't collapse in the middle of the department floor. My knees threatened to give way beneath the weight of my new strength, but somehow I willed my legs to carry me to safety.

I worked at Jeannette's desk for the rest of the day while I recovered. When I returned to my cubicle to shut down my computer, Mr. Williams was gone, but Renee was thrilled to see me.

"Bob's afraid you're mad at him. He's been worried about it all day. I can't believe you said that!" She was looking at me with a new admiration.

I didn't feel worthy of admiration or even remotely like a victor. I simply felt free of the weight I'd been carrying. Someone had seen the distress of the terrified schoolgirl and instead of cursing at me had directed me to safety. Now that little girl on the school yard was learning to talk back. My identity was no longer rooted in being "nice."

The dream and my response were never spoken of after that. And I was never again called into Mr. Williams's office to arrange a piece of clothing or pick up a paper clip.

I was finding my strength.

CHAPTER 9

Letting Go of Mother of the Year

My counselor's office felt warm and familiar. Deep burgundies and mellow shades of tan set off against mahogany and wrought iron. I sat on the overstuffed couch and admired the soft sunlight streaking through the plantation shutters. Alongside the books on her shelf were family photos and various pieces of art.

As she closed the door and took a seat across from me, she seemed genuinely happy to see me. And not just because I'd referred numerous people to her practice. Even though I paid her to be my traveling companion, there was a comfortable ease in our relationship. Then, like we were old friends, she asked, "So what's going on?"

My first experience with professional counseling was at nineteen. From the start, I'd loved it. I'd worked through much of my "big" stuff long ago and now just connected with my counselor occasionally, when I felt unable to navigate something specific. It had been years since I'd met with her, but she knew my story. I felt excited in spite of my "stuckness."

As is my pattern, I began speaking nervously. Rambling about this and that thing that was bothering me. She listened patiently, nodded appropriately, and took notes. As I stopped to take a breath, she paused and looked intently at me. I understood her cue and inhaled slowly and deeply, then exhaled. I needed to breathe.

After I gathered myself, she continued. "What else?"

"I'm terrified of what will become of my kids. I'm afraid I'm going to mess them up terribly." This was a strange thing for me to say because I had no idea I'd been feeling this way.

She probed some more. "Tell me about your kids. Do they seem to be moving in a dangerous direction?"

That was the thing. There were no outward signs of trouble, but my mothering had gotten off to a rocky start, and I was beginning to figure out I had very little control.

My journey toward motherhood began with a lie.

It didn't seem like a lie at the time. I felt like I knew something no one else knew. I knew God wanted me to be a stay-at-home mom and he would miraculously work it out in his timing. So when Richard put his arm around me as I held the newborn of a friend and made this proposal—"We could start trying now if you're willing to work part time"—I said yes.

What I meant was, "No, I'm not willing to work part time, but I'll have figured out a way to stay home by the time we have the baby, so . . . yes, let's start trying." But I kept that to myself. It turns out that is not only immature, but it's not a great way to build trust in a marriage, either.

And it seems I did not have some divine knowledge of the future. A year later I had a beautiful baby boy . . . and a job.

"So you're going back to work tomorrow and you haven't found a babysitter yet?" My friend Leah looked genuinely concerned.

Her statement wasn't exactly true. I hadn't actually looked for a babysitter and that had negatively impacted my ability to find one. Three months earlier, Leah and I had both given birth to our firstborn children, and my first day back at work was the day I'd been dreading. The day I had believed I could avoid by manipulating God. In spite of my desperate prayers and monumental denial, I needed to return to work.

From the early days of our marriage, I had wanted to turn in my business suits for more domestic attire. This was partly because I wanted to be a mom, but definitely because I was unhappy at work. My biggest fear was staying in the workforce after having children. My second biggest fear was being stung by a bee. Both turned out to be less painful than I'd anticipated, but not without some unnecessary drama.

Leah volunteered to babysit until I found someone permanently. Crisis averted. At least that crisis. Over the years there were numerous others. Like the time our firstborn, Caleb, fell down a full flight of stairs on his first birthday, or the day he sprayed bathroom cleaner in his eyes. There was the time we answered the front door to find Caleb accompanied by a stranger asking if he was ours. Apparently said stranger had been driving past our house, saw a toddler pushing a toy truck down the road by himself, and felt something was awry. Good guess.

There were the battles of wills and the broken bones (unrelated to each other) of our middle child, Cade, and losing our youngest, Madison, in the mall.

In spite of it all, I'd surprised myself with how much I loved being a mom. Not in the way many of my friends enjoyed it. I didn't particularly like talking about parenting. I just liked being a parent. I hated crafts and didn't have the energy to make my own diaper wipes or puree my own baby food. I didn't enjoy moms' groups. If I was getting free childcare for a few hours, I was going shopping, not to church.

I loved my kids and they knew I loved them. As they got older, we began a tradition of asking a "question of the night" at the dinner table. The question one night was, "What do you think is the best job in the world?" Each of our three kids went first and when it was my turn, our middle child smiled at me.

"Mom, it has to be something besides being our mom, because we know that's the best job." That hadn't been what I was going to say, but he was right. Being their mom was by far the best job in the world. But even better was that he knew how much I loved it. How much I loved him.

So why was I suddenly panicking about my parenting?

Well, there were some deficiencies. Let's just say I'm not highly domestic. My kids were never going to rave about my cooking. There was a brief period when I was trying to improve in this area and I went to a cooking class. I came home with a couple of good recipes. From that time on, whenever I cooked, my kids asked, "Did you learn this in your cooking class?"

Once Cade raved about my lasagna. It was Stouffer's. I'd never made homemade lasagna in my life.

I couldn't maintain a chore chart to save my life, and cleaning regularly was not a high priority. And I would never be accused of overparenting. I did not fit the mold in an age of helicopter parents.

Once, on a safari in Kenya, our guide enlightened us on the parenting skills of giraffes. "They're beautiful, graceful creatures," he marveled. "But they're terrible parents." Because they have long necks and can see their offspring from a great distance, they often walk away, leaving a fair amount of space between them and their calf. Unfortunately, it doesn't matter if you can still see your baby giraffe if you're not fast enough to get to it before the lion does. I felt more like a giraffe parent.

I'd invested heavily in a particular technique of parenting. This method came with a guarantee, and that's what I was looking for. If I did everything correctly, I was told, I could be assured they would turn out to be healthy, well-adjusted children who grew into successful, godly adults. I read the book and followed the instructions. I couldn't understand how any sane person wouldn't want to follow this method.

Then I read one more book. After that I found that most books on parenting only made me feel worse about myself and created chaos at home as I tried to reorganize everything around a new and improved strategy. I couldn't make myself fit into what seemed to be the prevailing wisdom on Christian parenting.

Most nights I prayed with the kids before they went to bed. And there were seasons where we regularly read Bible stories together. Very short seasons. Follow-through was never my strong suit. As the kids learned to read, I bought them their own devotional books, hoping they were better at sustaining patterns than I.

Unlike most of the other mothers at my kids' school, I did not pack my kids' lunches. I told them it was because they needed to learn responsibility. My responsible offspring would come home disgusted with the kids who depended on their parents to provide them with a lunch. "Those kids are never going to make it in the world," they would complain as they shook their heads condescendingly.

I did feel a little guilty that my deficiency was getting passed off as good parenting. But I got over it.

And then there were the lessons I was teaching my daughter. By the time Madison arrived, I'd actually begun to enjoy working. I enjoyed being a working mom. I once shared that little tidbit with a women's group where I was speaking. That was a mistake. More than one woman approached me after my address with a look of concern and a word about how my children needed me. One of them clearly thought I must not have been telling the truth. She put her arm around me and began her story with, "Well, dear. I had the *privilege* of staying home with my kids . . ." I don't know what she said after that, but it didn't matter because that was obviously the point she wanted me to take home. I understood this woman's passion to be an attentive parent. I wanted the same thing. But I was beginning to see that God had different paths for different women and I was trying to follow mine.

As a writer and consultant, much of my work time was spent in my home office. One morning when Madison was four years old, she entered my office with determination. She was wearing a dress and her best sandals. In her right hand was her LeapPad and in her left, a coffee cup full of water. I watched with amazement and curiosity as she situated herself in an office chair. After a deep sigh, she looked up at me and announced, "We're just two ladies workin' in the office."

Then she commenced with a busy morning of Dora the Explorer games and a couple of mugs of water. I could not have been more proud. Even with the tinge of shame.

While I felt comfortable with my balance between work and the rest of life and my kids all seemed to be thriving, I still questioned myself. I had very few examples of Christian women who worked outside the home, let alone had a career. Even fewer pastors' wives. And while I could confidently point to my well-behaved, well-adjusted young children, who was to say there wasn't some pain, some neglect hidden deep down in their psyche that wouldn't emerge until it was too late?

Perhaps that was the reason I found myself in my counselor's office. That and the fact that one of our kids had recently filled out his first-day-of-fourth-grade questionnaire with the following response:

I wish my mom was less stressed out all the time.

Maybe my work/life balance wasn't as solid as I'd thought. Or maybe my depression wasn't as under control as I'd envisioned. Or maybe I had been unusually irritable the morning he was asked to complete the inane worksheet and I was flipping out over nothing. Whatever the reason, I needed help.

As I recounted my fears in rapid succession, my counselor smiled. "Did your parents make any mistakes in the process of raising you?" she asked rhetorically. I didn't need to respond, I simply smiled.

"Look where your journey took you. You're a healthy, vibrant, loving adult. Do you think your kids might be able to survive your mistakes and step into their own journey?"

She had a point. Still, I felt a protest forming in the depths of my gut. "But I don't want them to repeat the painful mistakes I've made. Even more, I don't want them to suffer for my mistakes. In fact, I don't want them to suffer at all!"

The last sentence echoed through the cavernous silence it created.

Having been released from the darkness of my mind, my fears had been exposed to light and now had the opportunity to be transformed into truth. The counselor waited as the truth of my own words began to grow and slowly sink back into my being.

"Faith is the most difficult thing you can give your children because it requires you to allow them to be in situations that require it."

And then she looked my demons in the face and called their bluff. "This isn't really about your kids, is it? This is about you learning to trust. And the best gift you can give your kids is to work out your own stuff as you walk the path laid out for you."

What emerged from those counseling sessions became my strategy going forward. I acknowledged the fear I had of doing it wrong. Of harming my children beyond repair. I affirmed my decision to not read parenting books and to, instead, keep working on my emotional and spiritual health. I resolved to stop trying to keep my kids from failure or hurt or disappointment and to instead model for them how to live a life of faith and authenticity. Even if that meant I was viewed as a failure. And I began to let go of the compulsion to never make a mistake. I decided I didn't want to live a life of fear. I would fail boldly.

I may not win any "Mother of the Year" trophies, but I brought all of myself.

CHAPTER 10

Letting Go of Making an Impact

I love to run. More accurately, what I do is something between jogging and running. Once I ran a half marathon. Old people and chattering women wearing makeup and designer shoes passed me, but nonetheless . . . I call myself a runner.

Running is something I do for fun and sanity. Unlike my husband, who runs out of duty and for the thrill of being done with the run, I solve problems when I run. I pray and work out emotions as I cruise along the coastal path near my home. Some days I see dolphins in the bay and, occasionally, whales. On those days I stop running and stand still and watch.

I haven't always lived by the ocean. For twenty-five years I lived in the desert, and I ran along a glorified canal we called a lake. Some days I would see dead fish floating next to the trash in the stagnant water. And during the spring I'd inevitably forget not to wear lip balm, and swarms of tiny white flies would meet their death on my lips. But those runs were no less transforming, even for their lack of salt-misted breezes.

On one particular run, I had a bone to pick with God. I was beginning to notice that plenty of people I knew (if not most) did not share my compulsion for personal and spiritual growth. Few of my peers had graced a counselor's office, let alone expended the effort and cash I had regularly shelled out. And from external observation, they seemed happier than I. All my internal digging had unearthed a slew of buried neuroses and hidden desires. And for what? So I could more accurately loathe myself and acknowledge what I lacked? If ignorance was bliss, my self-knowledge was torture. I wanted to know if it was worth it.

The nice thing about running is that you can do it to a sound track. And all of life is better when you have a sound track. Wouldn't it be great if you could cue motivational music for that presentation at work? Or a silly song for when the dog has thrown up in her kennel and your two-year-old is playing in it? I just think it might help me know which emotion to feel other than murderous rage.

On this particular day, God used my sound track to punctuate his answer as we were discussing the meaning of my life. More accurately, I was whining. I had a few complaints I wanted to send to the Manager.

First of all, growth was more difficult, more painful, and much slower than I had anticipated. I felt there should be something in the brochure about that. Secondly, not everyone seemed required to complete the same series of tests required of me, and that didn't seem fair. And thirdly, I had been under the impression the high levels of energy I'd expended would result in a proportionately large payout. Preferably distributed in greater recognition, influence, or spiritual status, but cash would also be acceptable. I didn't want to appear ungrateful, but I feared I'd read the memo incorrectly and might be pursuing the wrong path. Better to cut my losses now.

I crossed the busy intersection that led to the "lake" as I formed my question into a prayer. "Lord, is it worth it? Does it matter to you that I'm working so hard at getting healthier emotionally and spiritually? Because nobody seems to notice, and I'm not sure I see any up side to this slow, painful process. I don't feel like I'm making an impact."

It was a sincere prayer. I was tired and confused. I had begun this process in the hopes of accomplishing something that mattered. Something of God, something big. Certainly God wouldn't have me go through the fire just to do the same things I was doing before. Would he?

My life was not on an upward trajectory. I had three small children at home, and I was working occasionally as a consultant. I enjoyed the freedom of choosing to say yes or no to ministry opportunities, and I had a more intimate relationship with God than I had ever experienced before.

But still I wondered... "What's it all for? Am I making any impact at all? Does my life matter?"

I don't know what I wanted, but I did know I wanted more. Not receiving but more giving. I was worried I wasn't doing enough to serve the poor or impact my community. After a number of years of spending extended amounts of time pursuing God, I had little to show for it externally. Yes, I was changing dramatically at a soul level, but it was taking longer than I'd anticipated. I'd pictured that I'd eventually live a more productive and impactful life after I got my internal stuff sorted out. I was beginning to question whether that would ever happen. A few weeks prior, I'd been with a group of women sharing some of my angst when one of them called me out: "Kelli, you need to let go of the idol of impact." That one hurt. But in a good way. I knew she was right, but I didn't know what to do with my desire to make an impact. I couldn't just wish it away.

That conversation was not in the front of my mind when I initiated my prayer, but God hadn't forgotten. As I made the turn onto the running path along the water, I became aware of the song playing on my iPod. It was a live Passion recording of "Jesus Paid It All." I had attended that event and could picture the thousands of college students standing in a field in Sherman, Texas, singing with all of their hearts. The recording included the sound of the crowd, and I could feel the excitement as if it were happening for the first time.

I noticed that my running pace was moving in rhythm with the song tempo, and I felt carried along, almost effortlessly. In my mind I saw the crowd, and as if in a dream, I became aware that I was running through this crowd toward the throne of Jesus. They were cheering. I was also aware they were cheering in direct response to the question I had asked moments earlier, "Does it matter?"

I was getting a picture of what it might feel like to enter heaven having run the race well. As I ran toward the throne, the crowd parted, and they smiled and cheered. On my iPod, the crowd was cheering and all my senses were engaged in this very real experience. But I was no longer an athlete running for a prize. I was a bride, overcome with affection, running faster and faster, spurred on by these virtual onlookers and the ever-growing desire to run into the arms of Jesus, the bridegroom. This was his answer. It mattered! The crowd of witnesses was affirming that my efforts mattered. No matter what the earthly outcome, the reward in heaven would be great.

If I had thought up this vision, it would have ended there. I would have been overjoyed. But what happened next confirmed that this was not some dream I'd created. It was truly God's answer. As I ran and the crowd parted and turned, I noticed they were no longer looking at me. The song on my iPod blared words of praise to Jesus who had raised my life from the dead. Over and over the words rang out, and I saw the throng turn toward the throne, singing this chorus in unison.

Then it hit me.

My transformation was the work of Jesus, and as I entered heaven, they were excited to see me so they could praise the one who had paid my debt.

It mattered. Not because of what it did for me and apart from any impact I imagined I produced. It mattered solely for the praise of the one who was working in me. I began to weep. I had been so selfish. Still trying to manipulate my way into creating my own meaning in life, I'd missed the whole point of transformation: whatever most honored Jesus.

CHAPTER 11

Letting Go of Super Spirituality

As I ran the steamy iron over my rarely worn, wrinkled slacks, tears streaked down my cheeks. I hated ironing. But that wasn't why I was crying.

This should have been a morning filled with excitement. One of those days you tell your children about later. But instead I felt ill equipped and spiritually unprepared for what lay ahead. In a few hours I would be ushered into then-governor Janet Napolitano's office with three other women, and we would be given the privilege of praying with her and for her.

Truth be told, I felt sorry for the governor. A person in her position should be getting prayed for by skilled pray-ers. Effective intercessors. I was neither. I was still puzzled by why they would send the B-team on such an important assignment. Nevertheless, it was too late to back out now.

Even a few months before, I would have felt great about participating, but my perception of my spiritual condition had taken a nosedive, and on this day I preferred to stay in bed. I liked it better when I felt like a spiritual giant.

Consolation and Desolation

Driving in northern Arizona from Phoenix always gets me thinking about what it would have been like to travel this terrain before the automobile . . . to cover the distance on horseback and discover the beauty over the next butte or on the other side of a mountain pass. The high desert is deceivingly hostile and unpredictable and can be unforgiving territory if you're unprepared.

On one trip to Sedona for our annual silent retreat, a carful of us seemed committed to talking as much as possible in anticipation of the impending period of quiet. Conversation was lively and fairly evenly distributed among each of us. At one point I noticed one of the women had gotten quiet, and I asked if she was okay. She looked suddenly tired as her gaze remained focused straight ahead.

"God just gave me a picture of my next year, and it's discouraging."

Wow. She was super spiritual. We hadn't even gotten to our destination yet, and she had already heard from God. We wanted to know more.

She went on to explain the process she had undergone over the last few miles of the journey. It seems that as we drove and talked, she began to notice the steep incline we were making. She felt the engine straining to provide the necessary energy to travel over the hill and experienced the tiredness of the seemingly endless nature of the climb. Just when she thought we were nearing the summit, we'd round a bend and the climb would continue. In the midst of this she observed the beauty of the mountain with its joyful absurdity of plant life sprouting out of rock.

She felt like this had been her journey over the last year. It had been a long, tiring climb up the mountain, not void of beauty, but harsh and seemingly endless. She hoped the next year would bring relief. That she would arrive at the top and be able to enjoy the view. As she was processing all this, we arrived at the top. The car approached the apex and the climb was over.

Yet it wasn't what she'd expected. Instead of a mountaintop with an expansive view of the verdant valley below, we'd come to a plateau, a long flat expanse of land. Barren and brown.

And this, she believed, was what her next year held. Bummer.

At the time of that conversation, I wondered why God would do that. Actually, I wondered if God *would* do that. But in the months that followed I had become acquainted with the terms *consolation* and *desolation*, and I was now painfully aware that the Christian life was not a linear journey where everything got continuously better.

I was experiencing desolation the morning of the prayer meeting with the governor. God did not seem near. And it wasn't for lack of trying on my part. I was trying to get near or trying to get him to come near—whatever the metaphor is. I wanted to be back to the place I'd been before, experiencing closeness, feeling filled with the Spirit, and enjoying being with God.

Instead, I felt dry and desperate.

I'd been on a journey of deeper healing over the last couple of years. One which I hoped would be the swan song of counseling in my life. A single event had opened up a wound I didn't know existed, and I believed this final process would, once and for all, clear out the last remnants of emotional scar tissue wrapped around my heart. As I processed my pain I reached a point where all that was left to do was forgive the person who had offended me. No easy task. And now I worried that all my efforts were just like the endless trail of treasure maps from *National Treasure*. Once I solved the riddle on my current map and risked my life to find the treasure, I would discover all it revealed was another clue.

I didn't want another clue. I wanted to arrive at my destination and settle in. I wanted to finally feel like an adult, unafraid of the frightened little girl who still had a grip on me. I wanted to reach a place of spiritual maturity where I spent my time making small tweaks to my character, not conducting complete renovations every couple of years.

I'd worked hard at this last battle. I'd fought the rage inside me, though it had led to fear and sadness and then back around to anger. This battle worked itself out in a brief profanity phase, which, according to my friends, was both frightening and hilarious. One afternoon as I sat in my friend Lisa's living room, the focal point of my anger came up in conversation and in a moment of frustration I blurted out, "He's such an ass!"

Lisa stared at me for a moment with perplexed amusement.

"Friend, I love you, but you are terrible at swearing." Then she burst out laughing and called for her husband, "Honey, come in here. You have got to hear this!" She coaxed, "Say it again, Kelli! It's so cute!" After that, my swearing days were numbered. Apparently a new, rougher vocabulary would not be the ticket out of my "good girl" bondage.

Then there was the issue of forgiveness. It threatened to be my undoing. After months and months of hard work, I remained unable to forgive. I was at a loss. For the first time, being the model counseling client, the star student, the premier "good girl" was not producing the desired result. I could not perform my way into a change of heart.

And that's where I found myself as I prepared to meet the governor. Only worse. In the days leading up to this event, the full weight of my humanness had descended on me. It was as if the facade of my perky smile and obedient nature had protected me from the reality of my depravity. With the demise of my primary strategy, the facade was crushed, exposing me as the broken person I was.

This wasn't the first time I'd experienced true brokenness, but there was a critical difference this time around. The first time, I'd had an eating disorder. Although I temporarily lost my smile and admitted I was a slave to rather un-good behavior, the treatment for my condition involved a repurposing of those skills. I learned to use my powers for good and not for evil. I found that the very behaviors that got me into trouble (a deep need to be liked, a propensity for following the rules, a well-developed sense of shame, and a drive to perform) could actually be refined, reshaped, and redeemed. In one sense, I'd simply found a healthier, more positive group of people to perform for.

That was all part of the process of maturing. But now I was at a hurdle, and I realized I did not possess the skills I needed to get over this hump. All I knew to do was to keep moving forward and hope God would reveal some fresh insight. A key that would unlock the door to a new way of living.

But I didn't have that yet. And I was going to pray with the governor now.

As I traveled downtown, I tried to pray, but my soul felt parched and weary. I needed God to come through; I didn't have the energy to perform in this environment. As I parked in the garage and walked toward the office building, my chest tightened and my mind froze. I entered the state building in a daze, and boarded the elevator up to my friend's office. She was a city council member, a friend to the governor, and the coordinator of this prayer meeting. Once in her office, I was introduced to the other two women, both pastors, who would be praying with us. I was the youngest. And I was quite certain I was the most broken. Perhaps I could excuse myself. "I'm sorry, ladies. I'm afraid I'm unable to forgive and am therefore a spiritual fraud, unqualified to join you this morning. And that's just the beginning. I'm really quite a mess. Thank you for considering me, but I'm afraid I'll be unable to participate."

I didn't say any of that. Instead, I followed the group to the reception area outside the governor's office and waited for her secretary to escort us in.

"The governor will see you now." That was exactly what I'd imagined she would say.

Because I wasn't really breathing and therefore not getting enough oxygen to my brain, I don't remember much about her office. I do recall that we sat in a circle in a number of large, comfortable chairs. I think they were red. The governor was friendly and relaxed. She seemed unhurried and genuinely appreciative that we would take time to encourage her.

There was a bit of small talk. She laughed about how her last name seemed difficult for people. How she was often referred to as Janet Neapolitan—as in the tricolored ice cream.

We each introduced ourselves briefly, and then my friend asked the governor how we could pray for her. This I remember well. She asked us to pray about the immigration issue. The day before she had been shown photos of a number of border crossers who had lost their lives in the desert. The photo that haunted her most was of a mother and her young child left in the desert to die on their way to a better life. They were most likely abandoned by the "coyotes" who had taken the mother's money and promised to escort her and her child to safety.

The governor said something to the effect of, "I don't know what the answer is, and I know it's a complicated, highly charged issue. But if we don't find any compassion when you look at that picture and don't feel any need to take some action to keep this from happening, then I don't know how we'll ever make any progress."

I know she could have been engaging in political posturing, but we were hardly high-powered constituents who had any influence in circles of power. She could have been so used to political speak that these kinds of persuasive mini-speeches were second nature. I remember hearing Charles Colson talk about the intoxicating pull of being close to someone in power. The governor of Arizona was hardly on the level of the President of the United States, but perhaps I'd fallen prey to this insidious temptation. I was a wretched grudge holder, after all, so giving in to the desire for power was an obvious next step.

But the truth is, I'm a romantic. I soaked it in. And I prayed like it was the deepest desire of her heart.

After we finished praying, we stood up, and she walked us to the door. We each shook her hand and wished her well as we exited. I made small talk with the other women as we walked through the hallway, into the elevator, and down to the large atrium at the entrance to the state building.

And, after I'd said goodbye, I ran. I couldn't wait to get out of there. I felt embarrassed and humiliated and worthless and angry. Why would God give me this opportunity today when I had nothing to offer? Why was I unable to make the changes I so desperately wanted to make? Why was all my hard work not producing the results I was used to? And, why did God now seem so far away?

I returned home drained and deflated. I relived my prayer in my head and felt appalled at its content, delivery, and lack of spiritual wisdom. Stupid! Stupid! Stupid!

Graciously and without prompting, God slowly began to speak to me.

As a means to hibernate and avoid thinking about my dreadful morning, I picked up the novel I was reading. It was one of the later books in the Starbridge Series. This brilliant series by Susan Howitch depicts the fictional English Anglican diocese of Starbridge throughout the late nineteenth and early twentieth centuries. All of the characters are beautifully broken and real. And in this particular installment, one of the priests explained that there were certain unhealthy parts of who he was that would not likely get fixed in this lifetime. Reading this passage a day earlier would have had me shaking my head in disgust at this fictional character. What a quitter! For me, emotional and spiritual growth was a non-optional, non-stop activity. But on this day, as I continued to read, God showed me something different.

I was waiting to live until I felt complete. I was striving to perfect myself so I could prove myself worthy of my calling. On some level I believed that I would ultimately earn my way into spiritual maturity. But on that day, a new hope began to take shape deep down in my soul. What if God knows my brokenness and accepts me in the middle of transformation? Not in a "That's just the way I am so deal with it" sort of way. But in the "I'm pursuing your path and trusting you to change my heart" way. What if I could unclench?

Later in the day I was reading another book. God gave me the same message. I wasn't fooling God. I quickly sat down to journal what God was saying to me. I acknowledged the truth of my situation. I was broken. I lacked the ability to forgive. I was unable to find reconciliation in other relationships, as well. God was already aware. I could stop trying frantically to fix it. I would continue to pursue God and live in the truth of my messiness.

I wept tears of joy. A burden had been lifted. A new way forward had been opened up for me, and God's silence had ended. I was not super spiritual, and I never would be.

Richard returned home to find me crying. Just like when he'd left me that morning. It is an adventure to be married to me.

CHAPTER 12

Letting Go of the Past

Throughout the years, professional and armchair psychologists alike had inquired about my history of sexual abuse. All the signs were there. I maintained, however, that I'd experienced no such thing. Certainly I would know if I'd been abused or molested. Yet even after years of analyzing the past, healing from wounds, and moving forward, I still had rocks left unturned.

The human mind is a complex thing, and the God who created it, so kind. As committed as I'd been to wholeness, perhaps I wasn't as strong as I'd thought. In his mercy, he continued to give me one piece at a time. And one afternoon over coffee, as I made an offhand remark about a story from my past, a dear friend made an observation that shifted all the right pieces into place. Images came rushing to the front of my brain, and I was overwhelmed to the point of breathlessness.

While my memories had not been suppressed, they had been altered. In my memory I was never the victim; instead, I was somehow to blame. But on that day, I remembered the event as a healthy adult, and my past was exposed.

As I sat at the outdoor café, I was transported back in time. And just like it was happening all over again, I could hear my friends laughing and shrieking on the shore as I lay on the cold, wooden, floating platform. My mind was fuzzy from the alcohol, but the midnight swim had sobered me enough to be aware of what was happening. I was naked, and I was being held down by the boy who'd brought me out here.

Learning How to Party

My freshman year in high school had just ended, and in a week my family was moving to a different city. At the last minute I'd organized a little going-away party for myself, given no one else had taken the initiative. To this point my little soirée was going better than expected. After hanging out at my house in the afternoon and downing a delicious meal prepared by my mom, I'd arranged for some older boys to meet us so I could cruise the town one last time. I told my parents we were going to watch a friend play softball, and my lie had been bought.

In just a few days, I'd be starting over in a new town, and I welcomed the change. In my new town, I'd be somebody new. I'd be the good girl I wanted to be. But tonight I was going out in style. A boy who'd earlier in the year rejected me was at the wheel of this carload of girls as we raced down the rural highway. I felt free and wild . . . and more than a little jealous. He was supposed to be with me tonight, but he was giving one of my friends a whole lot of attention.

After our first date, last fall, he hadn't called me again. I'd heard through the grapevine it was because I said no to his advances that night. I thought that was what I was supposed to do, but it cost me, and I was confused about the social cues.

I wised up as the year progressed, and the spring had brought a sudden surge in popularity for me. Just a lowly freshman, I found myself embraced by upper classmen as I was swept away into a world of teenage parties. I never really consented to this life, but here I was, thanks to a series of small yeses designed to keep me from embarrassment and rejection.

The move from innocence to lost innocence came in such a perky package. It's no wonder I missed it. Earlier that spring I'd been sitting around the table playing a card game with my family, when a car pulled into the driveway and my friend Kim bounced out and ran up the sidewalk to ring the doorbell. When I answered the door, she proceeded to invite me to drive around with her and her friends, who happened to be a group of senior guys.

Back in the day in rural Iowa, that's what we did—we drove around. I don't know why.

I was nearly a head taller than Kim, but what she lacked in height she made up for in energy and personality. She was a force with her jet black hair—long and straight with perfect bangs that shaped her tiny face. She had bright white teeth that were frequently on display with her infectious smile. She was a year older than me, and I wanted to be just like her. So her appearance at my door was like getting a personal invitation to the next level of social status. As a freshman I was being invited by a popular sophomore girl to get in a car with a couple of senior guys.

My parents consented to an hour of cruising, and I raced out without looking back. The car door opened as I approached, and I found myself invited to sit in the backseat between two boys I didn't know. I smiled shyly. Kim took her place in the front seat between two other boys, and we were on our way.

I'd been looking forward to hanging out with Kim, but now I had to make conversation with these strangers who didn't appear to be conversationalists. The feeling of freedom was dissipating, and I immediately wanted to go home.

Kim practically bounced with enthusiasm as we drove through town. Each boy in the car was mesmerized by her, and I wasn't sure what my role was, other than to go along for the ride.

"So will you party with us, Kelli?" She pleaded as she turned around to look at me with a twinkle in her eye. Frankly, I thought we were partying already. A couple of teenagers driving around without our parents—this was a party.

"Sure," I responded with a smile. I certainly didn't want to stop a party. But I did find myself curious about what that meant exactly.

"I knew it!" she exclaimed with admiration as she returned to face the front. "I told these guys, 'I know someone who will party with us.' This is so great!"

I was puzzled as to why this would be such a hard sell, but thrilled she seemed so impressed with my willingness to go along.

"Alright, let's go boys," she commanded. "She's going to party with us." I marveled at the hold she had on this carful of young men. Her charisma was hypnotic, and I couldn't help but be amazed. But I was still confused by the goal of this evening. Were we going to turn up the radio? Drive fast? What was this partying of which Kim spoke so enthusiastically. I was unprepared . . .

For life.

The driver pulled the car into a convenience store and parked out of sight of the cashier. I could feel the tension building as the boys shared nervous glances. As the driver (the oldest of the crew) exited the car, Kim turned to give me the lowdown. "He's going to go buy us some beer. He's got a fake ID."

The wave of shame sucked the air from my lungs. I fought to keep my face from betraying me as I sensed my cheeks getting hot. How had I not known what was happening? How had I not understood the meaning of *party*? And now what was I going to do?

Kim seemed to sense my hesitancy, and she continued to encourage me. "You're still in, right? This is going to be so great. You're so cool." Her words were straight out of the *How to Avoid Peer Pressure* handbook. It was just like the scripted peer-pressure scenes I'd watched on many after-school specials as a child, but somehow I was still unprepared.

It never occurred to me to say no. Somewhere deep inside I knew my strategy. Lie low. Act natural. Don't make any sudden movements. Exit the scene slowly and calmly without embarrassing yourself.

Our beer runner emerged from the store with a bag, and the car went silent. We all held our breath as he opened the door and calmly placed the bag on the floor. No one spoke or made eye contact as he turned the key in the ignition, shifted into reverse, and slowly exited the parking lot.

All hell broke loose as we drove away. They all whooped and hollered like they'd just won the hog-tying competition at the state fair. Which, incidentally, was probably in their future.

Within seconds, the first can was being opened and passed around. When it got to me, I took a sip and passed it to the boy next to me. One small yes. No visible damage.

But something had changed inside of me that night. I felt afraid and alone, and I believed I did not have the skills necessary to navigate the next phase of my life. My father had taught me to "always act like you know what you're doing," and that was how I intended to cope. I honed my ability to perceive what was required to fit in without embarrassment in any social setting and did whatever it took. I tried to stay under the radar as much as possible, quietly observing as I withdrew into myself. If someone engaged me in the conversation, I was ready to respond in a way that ensured my continued participation and good favor within the group.

Which Is How I Ended Up Here . . .

I was employing the same strategy at my going-away party. Stay under the radar, don't do anything stupid, act like you know what you're doing. I'd had a bit more than a sip to drink, and I was feeling mellow and tired. My plan was a fun ride through the countryside, return home safely, go to sleep, and then wake up and start my new life. But that wasn't what everyone wanted.

"Let's go skinny dipping!" my pseudo-date suggested to me above the music as we cruised through the countryside. Just ahead was the quarry-turned-swimming-hole where my friends would soon be gathering on hot summer days. It wouldn't take much to climb the chain-link fence and find ourselves on our own private beach.

"I don't think so," I replied calmly. I assumed he was joking.

I wasn't alone in the car, and my friend, who had been receiving all the attention from my former homecoming date, was up for anything, so he repeated the question to her.

"Yes!" she agreed enthusiastically. She giggled with glee at the prospect. I wondered what was wrong with me that I had so much hesitancy. I could see myself being replaced right before my eyes, and I wasn't quite ready to be obsolete.

So that was it. I would have to consent or my night would be ruined. I pretended to be suddenly thrilled.

Once on the sandy beach, even the diehard enthusiasts seemed hesitant. It was a cold May evening, and the reality of disrobing in front of each other suddenly felt awkward. The boys agreed to go first. Not surprisingly, they were more committed to this adventure. They stripped down to their underwear and sprinted into the murky water.

I looked around at the faces of the girls standing on the beach. Few of them had expected to be in this situation when they agreed to come to my party. None of them knew the Kelli who hung out with senior boys or who drank cheap liquor and lied to her parents. Most of them looked a bit shell-shocked. And most of them had no intention of stripping down and entering the cold water. I envied them. I, of course, would have to go because I had gotten us into this mess and my friend had called my bluff.

I walked to the edge of the sand with a few of the other foolish girls, and we slipped off our shorts and T-shirts as we sunk into the water. I just wanted it to be over.

Perhaps fifty yards from shore was a floating platform, anchored to the bottom of the quarry/lake. We called it "the raft." There, the water was deep enough to dive, and in the summer it was where all the older, cool kids hung out. The boys were already there, and they called for us to join them. We swam over to the raft and hoisted ourselves up onto the platform, unsure of what to do as we stood there, underwear clad, cold and dripping wet.

For most of the group, that little party on the raft lasted a very short time. I imagine my "date" had asked his friends to leave so we could be alone. Or maybe he just got lucky. Either way, we were left unaccompanied as everyone else soon swam back to shore and got dressed. They didn't notice that back on the platform I was trying to wriggle free without causing a scene. That I was objecting to what was happening.

I'd finally reached the point where I could say no. Only he wasn't listening. And he was stronger than me.

I said no, but nobody believed me. And I believed it was my fault.

A New Vision

The memory had always been with me, but I had never seen it for what it was. In one evening nothing and everything had changed.

Surprisingly, as the reality set in, I felt relief. I wasn't the wild child I'd been trying to hide. Certainly I'd made some bad decisions, and I had caused my own share of pain. But I had said no, and that mattered. A new vision of myself was set in motion, and I experienced a sense of hope in the midst of deep sadness for innocence lost. The scars of my past were quickly loosening their grip on my life.

CHAPTER 13

Letting Go of the Ideal Marriage

Ours is not a classic love story. Unless your idea of a classic love story is based on any John Hughes film from the 1980s. Then, we're classic. (If you're not familiar with John Hughes, think *Pretty in Pink* and *Sixteen Candles*.)

Part of me imagined I'd marry a musician. Actually, I didn't give my future mate's occupation much thought. In hindsight, that was an egregious oversight. I just wanted my Prince Charming to come along and sweep me off my feet.

I met Richard Gotthardt at church, weeks after moving to Arizona my sophomore year of college. With less than twenty students in the small college ministry, it was impossible to stay under the radar. Richard was sociable and the only male in the group unafraid to ask a girl out. I did not want to be asked out by Richard. That fact only spurred him on and he set out to overcome the hurdles I'd placed in his way.

Primarily, I was dating someone else. It wasn't serious and my "boyfriend" lived across the country, but he was a convenient excuse for not dating other guys.

Richard, on the other hand, was ever present and persistent. While I immediately relegated him to the friend zone, I found myself increasingly comfortable around him. He was smart and funny and a great listener. His insights were deep and creative, and I loved how his mind worked.

Also, he was conveniently codependent.

I was a mess. Despite my desire to follow Jesus and my connection to the local church, a full-blown eating disorder, occasional drinking binges, and fraternity parties secretly characterized my life. Richard was warned by responsible people that I was trouble, which continued to add to my appeal.

To answer your question, yes, I still considered myself a "good girl." I despised my own behavior but felt powerless to stop it. In many social circles, I still played the part, and I was torn between the little girl who wanted to please and the person whose destructive behavior was oozing out from years of suppressed emotion and the self-loathing I could no longer control.

As I later learned in treatment, food is the good girl's drug. Case in point. I once ate an entire loaf of raisin bread in front of my grandparents. My grandma was thrilled! She'd been telling me I was too skinny and felt proud to be the one to fatten me up. Not only could I use my drug without being criticized, I was affirmed for it.

But I was dying on the inside, and I wanted help. Clearly I needed to up the stakes in order to get rescued. My life and emotional pain were getting out of control, and compulsive eating did not seem to be enough of a red flag to people. My drinking was both a cry for help and an indicator of how deeply I despised myself.

Richard was around when I was sick, and he kept in touch while I was in treatment, and he picked me up from the airport when I returned to Phoenix to begin my recovery. Within six months we were dating.

In this early phase of our relationship, I had all the power. After a month I'd broken it off and shut off my emotions completely. I shared my hope that we could go back to being friends. That wasn't going to happen. Over the next three months, we didn't speak to each other.

And then without warning, Richard got over me. Maybe he just gave up, but suddenly I felt loss. After a few months of no communication, he said a few words to me. My heart melted. There just wasn't anyone in my life with whom I connected so powerfully.

A few weeks later we were on a double date. We weren't dating each other, but we were together with our respective dates. It was supposed to be a study date, but Richard was too smart to study so he convinced us all to see a movie. As the opening credits appeared, the emotions of the last months all surfaced at the same time. I excused myself to use the restroom, cry my eyes out, and ponder my next move. I was gone awhile, and when I exited the women's restroom, there was Richard leaning against the opposite wall.

Okay, that's kind of classic.

After a lengthy conversation, we decided to get back together. We returned to watch the end of the movie with our respective dates, then left the movie together. It was less awkward than it sounds. No one was surprised we ended up together.

We were married a little over a year later. So, like I said. Classic love story.

And then the "ever after." Or, what we call our first marriage. When you've been married as long as we have, you've weathered a number of major shifts in your relationship. The big shifts usually require a renegotiation of roles, a letting go of "what was" and willingness to move forward into a "new" marriage. This is where we began.

The First Marriage

There were years of seminary when I worked to support Richard, then a house and babies and ministry growing pains. Our marriage continued to strengthen. Five years in and we were hitting our stride.

Richard and I were the ideal ministry couple. We were both strong leaders, both had speaking skills, and both had a passion and vision for ministry. Richard could preach. I could help lead worship. Richard could develop the larger ministry structures, and I could facilitate leader training sessions. Richard could lead the male group leaders, and I could lead the female group leaders. We led short-term teams overseas together. We conducted premarital counseling together.

It was perfect.

Except it wasn't.

In the faith tradition from which Richard and I hail, couples are supposed to be involved in ministry together. And if your husband is the pastor, as his wife you are expected to be not only his number-one fan, but also the model parishioner. And not just in character and godliness, but also in adhering to the highest membership requirements of the church.

Sometimes things happen so gradually that you don't notice the way they are no longer working. And sometimes you don't know any other way so you're not sure what to do about the dissonance. "I'm probably just being picky or selfish," you think. "Or maybe I'm just weak or have a low capacity for leadership. Certainly this is my issue." At least, that's how it worked for me.

Shame.

"This is what I'm supposed to do."

Should.

Until I couldn't do it anymore. And that's how this little story began. Me quitting ministry. It took some time to find our center again. But after a few years, I regained my health and my perspective and I had energy and I was ready to get active. Exactly my stated purpose for quitting in the first place. See, I *did* know what I needed. And thus began our second marriage.

The Second Marriage

As Richard noticed my improved mood and energy levels he began presenting me with opportunities to serve. No big commitments. All in areas where I was gifted. From a leadership standpoint, it was both loving and brilliantly executed.

But no matter how well suited I was for the task or how sweetly Richard asked, I almost always felt a knot in the pit of my stomach and a tightening in my chest as soon as the request was made. It made no sense.

I concluded that I'd simply gotten soft and lazy in my season of recovery. What if this was exactly what Richard feared when I stopped serving? I imagined this was a course taught in seminary—"Getting the Most from Your Volunteer Labor."

Rule number one: Don't let them stop. Once they stop, they'll begin to enjoy the downtime and they may never return—they'll be lost to you forever.

I didn't want to be lazy or selfish but I'd also spent the last couple of years learning to listen to God. I'd learned that just because I *could* do something didn't mean I *should* do it. I knew that no was a legitimate response. But now it seemed the only response I knew.

From Richard's perspective, I hadn't told the truth. When I stepped away from serving, I'd clearly stated it was for healing. For a season. It looked to him like I had simply wanted out and hadn't been up front with him. It didn't help that I couldn't articulate a reason for my reticence to serve. And then he noticed something alarming. I got excited about certain ministry ideas—but none of them were with him. This felt like a slap in the face. I had the ability, the giftedness, and the passion to serve as a leader, and it would be possible to find a place where I could use that in his ministry arena. But I was actively choosing not to serve next to my husband. How selfish was I?

Why wasn't I drawn to using my skills in a way that allowed me to more tangibly support my husband or, at the very least, spend more time with him? Wasn't it better for a marriage if we had a common ministry focus and experience?

I thought about the way women lived for centuries before this one. They sucked it up and did what they were supposed to do. What about the women I'd worked with in South America and Africa? They had very little freedom to say no. I wasn't being forced into a bad marriage or denied anything I needed. If I'd been able to articulate a dream, Richard might have given me a clean slate to pursue it. As it stood, the only thing I seemed sure of was what I didn't want.

I had no explanation for how a "good girl" who wanted to do the right thing, was pursuing God and trying to make everyone happy, could not get happy about doing this thing that she perceived a godly wife should do. For years I searched for ways to make it work.

Richard and I wrestled with my role in serving in churches where he was on staff. I felt ashamed of not being the wife I wanted to be or the wife my husband wanted me to be. And I was growing increasingly unhappy with him as well.

Then the tension reached a breaking point and I spoke an even more decisive no. No, I would not join with him in ministry today and no, it might never happen. Also, no, I would not attend events or functions or services just because I was a pastor's wife. Just no.

I desperately wanted to move forward, but I also knew I couldn't simply acquiesce after all the work I'd done to integrate my inner self and my interaction in the world. I hoped one day to participate alongside Richard, but that day was not today and I couldn't pretend. I would have to release the image of an ideal marriage in order to get to the root of my angst. And unfortunately, without any say in the matter, Richard would have to let go as well.

I felt I was hurtling myself backward. No was not going to bring me freedom, but I didn't believe yes would either. So I donned an invisible but highly effective shell around my heart while I attempted to collect my thoughts and find a way toward healing. It was too late before I discovered my protective shell couldn't be isolated or managed. One day I looked down to discover that, much like the boy Eustace in C.S. Lewis's *The Voyage of the Dawn Treader*, I was covered in the thick, ugly skin of a dragon and I knew I needed help.

In this fifth book of the Chronicles of Narnia, Eustace puts on the skin of a dead dragon and is unable to free himself. As he struggles to escape the stifling scales, Aslan approaches and offers to help. This is good news, but it will not come without pain. Aslan must use his sharp claws to rip open the dark covering in order to free Eustace from his protective prison.

I have always loved that picture, which is probably why God used it when he intervened to offer a picture of hope. One afternoon as I sat alone with God, he held up a mirror to show me my condition. I didn't recognize myself in my prickly skin and yet I felt afraid of what would happen to me if it was removed.

As I watched him move closer to the dragon-like me in my vision, I saw the scales being ripped from me—painfully and beautifully—from top to bottom. I winced as Aslan's claws broke through the armored skin. What I expected to see was a weak, ashamed, emaciated self inside, but instead, a brilliant light emerged. Pure, radiant, penetrating brightness. And there I was in the midst of the light. Strong and hopeful. Full of love. Ready to give.

This was God's plan for me, but it would not happen in one dramatic event. I knew it would require work. And I would have to say yes to something.

My first step was to stop blaming Richard for the dissonance I experienced in discussions about ministry. I started taking responsibility for my own dreams and passions without diminishing his. Then I began to explore God's unique path for me and the ministry desires slowly opening like a cautious bud. I came alive as God brought opportunities to travel and connect with godly men and women and create space for silence and slowing that brought restoration and renewal.

But even as my enjoyment of God deepened and I found my work and ministry to be energizing and affirming, there remained a disconnect in our marriage. Not a chasm and not on most issues. But on this very sensitive topic of church and ministry we tiptoed around each other. So we kept striving to move toward each other.

And then in an unexpected series of difficult discussions, perspective shifts, and courageous actions, something shifted. Aslan's claws ripped off both of our masks and introduced us to a new experience of oneness. This marked the beginning of our third marriage.

The Third Marriage

Our first marriage was characterized by codependence. Our second marriage, by independence—mostly on my part. (I rarely miss an opportunity to give the pendulum a good, hard swing in the opposite direction.) But this third marriage is a move toward interdependence. Toward oneness. And it is beautiful.

We are still two imperfect people with strong ideas and stubborn wills who are trying to make life work as we pursue intimacy with God and each other.

People outside our marriage don't always agree with how we define our roles or interact around ministry. For instance, a while back I was experiencing a deep dissonance in my soul while worshiping in our home community. In most churches, they appreciate when the wives of the pastors also attend the church. It really doesn't seem too much to ask. But this was a unique season for me. I was in grad school, my kids were older and no longer sat with me during our church gathering, and I longed to experience a different tradition. This was not church shopping fueled by consumerism or a need to get something more from church. There was an ache in my soul.

Richard and I discussed my desire and acknowledged the potential fallout. It was not ideal for me to find life in an expression of community outside that of my husband's. It wasn't Richard's first choice. But he had journeyed long enough to understand that God speaks to each person in a unique voice. Even more, God speaks to us differently in different seasons of our life. Richard gave grace and freedom for me to follow God's voice. Even when that freedom might cause discomfort for him and others.

I began attending a nearby Anglican church on Sunday mornings and it was even more life-giving than I had hoped. The liturgy and the rootedness wrought by centuries of wisdom brought me face-to-face with God in new ways, which was what my heart longed for in this season.

After twenty-five years we may finally be getting this thing down. I'm still aware of my unique passions and gifts and my desire to pursue whatever path God sets me on. But I am also awakening to a strong desire to find ways to creatively integrate my life and ministry with Richard's. In this new season I am less concerned with the form I experience on a Sunday morning and more drawn to prayer and connecting with people. Richard and I now worship in the same community—because it is where God is calling us both.

And I am free. Free to say no. Free to say yes. In that vein, I'm still learning what to hold on to because it's part of God's unique plan for me, and what to let go of because I'm gladly joined to another, and that is clearly a part of God's beautiful plan for me.

It's messy. And terrifyingly freeing.

Living Out

Lord, make me an instrument of thy peace.

—St. Francis

For we are God's masterpiece. He has created us
anew in Christ Jesus, so we can do the good things
he planned for us long ago.

—Ephesians 2:10 (NLT)

CHAPTER 14

A New Heart

Letting go is tiring. You would think it would have a load-lightening effect. The relief of carrying around less weight. Maybe that's how it feels when you easily release your grasp on lesser things, but I had not let go passively. I was tired from all the wrestling. By this time I understood that time in silence and rest was valuable, but so was action. Contemplation and prayer without action produced neither piety nor lasting change and I knew it was time to leave the nest. But I was so tired.

I had more emotional and spiritual strength than I ever remembered experiencing, but I found it difficult to envision participating in much activity. It wasn't depression. I wasn't overworked. I was getting plenty of rest. But this was real physical exhaustion. I couldn't lift a basket of laundry without getting short of breath. Which, while a great excuse to not do laundry, was also somewhat alarming.

And that's when I knew it was time.

As a junior in high school, a routine sports physical uncovered a heart murmur. Further testing revealed I had a fairly common heart abnormality called mitral valve prolapse, but also a very leaky aortic valve. No immediate response was necessary, just a commitment to regular check-ups and the realization I would eventually need to have it replaced—probably between the ages of forty and fifty. I was sixteen at the time, and I couldn't fathom being that old. I assumed my life would be winding down by then anyway.

I had faithfully monitored my heart through the years and now it had become apparent I would need to have the valve replaced. I was just shy of my fortieth birthday.

I met with my cardiologist, and he confirmed my amateur diagnosis. Because this was something I'd known was a possibility for twenty years, and a number of family members had undergone open-heart surgery, the reality of it didn't sink in during that first meeting. Richard and I met the next week with the cardiothoracic surgeon who would perform the operation, and he assured us this was an extremely easy surgery for him. His confidence and laissez-faire demeanor rubbed off on both of us, and we left feeling like it was no big deal. My biggest concern was my trip to Dubai for a speaking engagement scheduled for five weeks after surgery. I wondered if I would be able to go. My surgeon assured me I would be fine. How serious could this be if I could be embarking on international travel in slightly more than a month?

The day of the surgery, Richard and I dropped the kids off at school and headed to the hospital to register. We sat across the desk from a perky young woman who meticulously recorded my information. Name. Weight. Height. Medical history. Payment information. Emergency contacts. It was all very surreal, but the reality was beginning to hit. This time tomorrow I would be out cold with my rib cage broken, my chest pried open, and my heart and lungs replaced with a machine while they carefully removed my faulty valve and replaced it with a healthier one from a dead pig.

But first I needed to make it through this day. Today's procedure was a heart catheterization where the doctor threads a long, thin tube (a catheter) through an artery or vein in your leg or arm into the heart. I responded well to the light anesthesia and slept blissfully through the internal inquiry into the chambers of my heart.

After that, blood tests, X-rays, and more blood tests. Then visits from my kids, my parents, some friends, my pastor, and most of my extended family. Finally the surgeon stopped by for some quick banter before the surgery. By this time, the reality was sinking in for Richard and he articulated it to the surgeon.

"I know you said this was a mundane surgery—the equivalent of removing tonsils for you, but to us this feels pretty major."

"Oh, it's a big deal," he replied affirmatively. "This is major surgery. Anytime you're cracking the chest open and stopping the heart, there's a level of risk involved." He seemed perplexed that we were just now coming to grips with this. I felt like he would have said, "Duh!" if it had been acceptable. Then I understood. All his posturing about the ease of the process was about his superior skill. To diminish the seriousness of the operation would be to diminish his expertise. And that was insulting. I didn't want to insult my surgeon.

At this point, I was numb to any nervousness. My emotions were muted, and I felt detached from reality.

A young male orderly came in to advise me he would need to help me shower. That seemed fairly awful, and I asked if perhaps my husband could help me instead. He agreed, and I breathed a sigh of relief. I would get to end this day with a modicum of dignity.

My surgery was scheduled for the crack of dawn the next day, so I nodded off early. When I awoke, Richard was sitting next to me, and my stomach was in turmoil. I wondered how I got nervous in my sleep, but the anxiety felt intense and suffocating. I turned to Richard and reached out for his hand. The nurse popped in to say she'd be back in a minute to take me to pre-op. I stuffed the urge to cry.

It was suddenly happening too quickly. A truncated goodbye with Richard and I was being wheeled into the operating room. As I entered, a nurse wondered aloud why I was still awake. The room was blindingly bright. Like a stainless steel showroom, spacious and cold.

The anesthesiologist arrived to work his magic, and I was out. Really, really out. They definitely don't want you coming to in the middle of this surgery. They make sure you're in a deep, deep sleep.

The next thing I remember is my eyes opening for a moment and Richard standing next to me. It's dark, and I can't speak because of the tube down my throat. I'm not sure where I am, but I desperately don't want Richard to leave. I squeeze his hand as hard as I'm able before I fall back into my trance.

"You need to wake up, sweetie." Someone is patting my arm. "We're going to sit you up." I'm disoriented and groggy. My throat is dry from the intubation tube that is still pushed down my throat. As they sit me up, I start to feel nauseous and my eyes widen as I begin to throw up. Still unable to speak I feel scared and embarrassed. The nurse sponges the vomit off my bloated body. I'm definitely awake. I've been under for seventeen hours, but I'm beginning to understand where I am and what's happening.

Eventually they pull the intubation tube, and I'm able to drink some hot tea to soothe my burning throat. I want to see Richard. He arrives a couple of hours later, and I don't want him out of my sight. I can't squeeze his hand hard enough. I'm so grateful to be alive and loved and—did I mention alive?

A New Decade

Recovery was much slower than I'd been led to believe. I was relatively young and in above average shape so I assumed I would be feeling back to normal in about six weeks. Especially since my doctors told me, "You'll be feeling back to normal in about six weeks." That was crazy talk. Or, at least, a very serious miscommunication. When I heard "back to normal" I heard "doing everything you'd been doing prior to surgery." This included running three or four times a week, grocery shopping, speaking, socializing, entertaining, mentoring, etc. Apparently, when my doctors said normal, they meant my rib cage would be less sore, my scars would be healing, I'd be able to breathe normally and probably drive for short periods of time. Whose normal is that?

Three weeks into my recovery I celebrated my fortieth birthday. I still became short of breath if I walked too quickly, my chest felt like I was wearing a lead vest, and my face was a pasty gray instead of its usual vibrant pink. Even so, I'd never felt more alive.

I love monuments and natural markers. The symbolism of entering my fifth decade of life with a new heart filled me with excitement and gratitude. I knew I would be different. God had been working internally to transform my frightened, angry, wounded heart into a strong, beautiful, loving heart. It had required a radical restructuring and the recovery proved more laborious than I'd hoped, but in the weeks of physical recovery I had time to reflect on the goodness and grace shown me. My strengthening physical heart was a tangible reminder of my internal change.

As planned, five weeks following open-heart surgery, I traveled to Dubai for a speaking engagement. I was still weak and in need of rest so I allowed myself to be cared for. I took advantage of wheelchair service in the expansive airport. I drank fresh juices twice a day. I slept whenever I had the opportunity and I used my words sparingly. Talking often required more energy and oxygen than I had to spare.

When the conference began I felt jet-lagged and tired. I asked for a stool on which to sit so I wouldn't pass out during my workshops, but I didn't need it. As each session began, I was infused with energy and words. Women from over forty countries and every continent but Antarctica had come together and it was quite literally a taste of heaven. And for the hour I was leading my workshop I had the energy of a twenty-year-old.

As soon as it was over, I'd be weak and shaky and need to sleep for a few hours. I knew I was not operating in my own power. I experienced the power of the Holy Spirit, and I never wanted to go back to operating solely in my own strength. This is how I began my fortieth year.

God was doing a new thing in me. I had a new physical heart, a renewed spiritual heart, and a sense of hope for what was ahead. I was finding a new song. A song of hope and freedom. A song of creativity and strength. A song that opened up my soul and created more and more space for serving and loving and giving.

CHAPTER 15

A Year of Abundance

As my interior life continued to deepen I found myself increasingly in need of intentional practices that might anchor me. One practice that emerged was asking God if there was a word, phrase, or verse that I should meditate on during the coming year. Some years the answer was yes and other years I didn't sense any clear directive. Either way I was fine. I didn't feel the need to put words in God's mouth, but I did enjoy having a plumb line from which to observe patterns. One year my word was *beauty*. Another, it was *surrender*. I felt comfortable with those words.

But the year after my heart surgery, God invited me to focus on the word *abundance*. I felt less comfortable with that word. I had already been experiencing abundance. Nine months after surgery I had completed a half marathon and I possessed more energy and creativity than I could remember ever having.

But the coming year looked to be a difficult one. I felt more and more disillusioned with this thing we called "church" and I rarely attended the morning gathering, choosing instead to gather with a small group of women as we learned together how to engage Scripture through meditation, art, music, prayer, and movement. But this life-giving group didn't erase the reality of the future. We knew layoffs were coming and there was a growing tension in both the staff and church members as the waiting dragged on.

As I meditated on this word, I used colored pencils to write it out in my sketchpad. This was another practice I had recently begun—drawing (more like doodling) as I prayed and processed my thoughts. I wrote *abundance* in big block letters and the word covered both the left and right sides of my open notebook. I immediately noticed that to the left of the spine were the letters A-B-U-N, which had no meaning, but to the right of the spine it spelled D-A-N-C-E. I hadn't planned this, but my heart leapt as I read it. A year of dancing seemed good.

As I continued to think and pray and doodle around the letters, the shape of a butterfly emerged. Another sign of goodness and new life. While not improving my artistic ability, this method of processing proved an effective way for me to connect my left and right brain and open myself to the Holy Spirit. Mysteriously, my anxieties for the year seemed to dissipate. Not because I had any more clarity about what the future held or even any assurance of positive outcomes. I was beginning to grasp an abundant life that held pain and difficulty. For the first time this seemed a real possibility.

I began memorizing Psalm 65 at that same time and out of it emerged an even clearer picture. Verse 11 says, "Even the hard pathways overflow with abundance" (NLT). This was not a God who wanted to harm me or who stood, detached, watching my life crumble because he knew it would be good for me in the end. No. This God was near in the tough pathways, the compressed dirt of a well-traveled road. Not only near, but at work creating beauty and goodness all around me—even when I feared I might be trampled.

And this is exactly what he did.

The Hard Pathway

Just a month after a butterfly emerged on my paper, Richard and I sat together at a special church meeting. The worship center spilled over with people this night. Not a single Sunday morning had seen this level of commitment in months. But between genuine concern and morbid curiosity, the pews were packed. Richard and I sat in the far right section as usual. I felt a subdued sense of calm. Not so much peace, as exhaustion and numbness covering an inner discontent and confusion that had been growing for quite some time.

I knew the contents of the meeting this evening. I knew the outcomes. I knew that soon my husband would be invited to take the stage and assure this wondering crowd that everything was going to be all right. Our senior pastor had been let go nine months earlier, and Richard had been pastoring and teaching and caring for the staff and the congregation ever since. While he didn't have an official title as the senior pastor, many told him they considered him as such. In fact, it wasn't uncommon for people who no longer attended our church to tell Richard they still considered him their pastor. That's what happens when you get to know my husband. You feel cared for in a way that changes you.

I looked down at the bright blue pew cushion I was sitting on, pews where I had sat for over twenty years. I glanced over at the aisle I had walked down to join my life to the man I sat next to tonight. The sanctuary where Richard had performed dozens of wedding ceremonies. The pulpit from which he had preached hundreds of sermons. The grand piano that had accompanied me on countless Sundays. The stage on which our kids had all stood to recite Bible verses at their school chapel services. The balcony stairs where they'd run up and down while they patiently waited for us to finish a meeting. This space held most of the foundational memories of my adult life.

There was an odd energy in the room. Everyone seemed aware something was about to change, but in a way they couldn't quite anticipate or prepare for. Friends greeted each other with smiles and hugs, but there was a hesitancy. An underlying sense that within an hour the laughter might feel irreverent or crass. Many had experienced meetings like this in this very building before, and they knew anything could happen.

I reached over to grab Richard's hand. He wrapped his hand around mine and squeezed back. I didn't turn to look at him, but I felt his heavy exhale. This amazing man next to me was the strongest person I know. To be sharing this experience was one of the proudest moments of my life. Even as I felt the rise of tears that would follow, I sensed the smile of God on us. The pervasive awareness of his presence and pleasure. Abundance.

The crowd stilled as the board of elders ascended the stage. Along with them were the three staff members who had been tasked with making the recommendations that served as the subject of this gathering.

Someone prayed, and then it began. A member of the elder board stood at the microphone, and then it was time for the big reveal.

"And now, ladies and gentlemen, the winners of tonight's reorganization are . . ." I'm quite sure this wasn't the introduction, but it is what I hear in my mind today.

I felt like the person who writes the winners' names on the Oscar cards. I knew what was coming, but this would make it real. I felt more and more detached from my body and I feared I might faint.

The first name was read, and a PowerPoint slide of her now-former ministry responsibilities was displayed. This was part business meeting, with the organizational charts and budget numbers, and part family meeting, with the announcement of staff who were being lovingly released to pursue God's best for them. That's how we talk about laying people off in the church. My first instinct was to clap, because that's what you usually do when someone announces a name in a setting like this. But not tonight. Who knew what was appropriate on a night like this one?

Then the second name. We'd sat at a local pizza place with this winner and his wife earlier in the week. We all knew at that point what was ahead, and we laughed and reminisced about our ministry years together. As with the first name, people were looking around, shaking their heads, unsure of how to respond.

The third name happened to be a member of the staff committee who had decided who got let go. But it was a bit of a setup because he already had another job at a church a few miles away. Regardless, it was a brief respite of not-so-bad news in the midst of an emotionally draining evening.

There was one more name to be read. I was definitely having an out-of-body experience. "And the last name is . . ." The air became eerily still, and I felt myself smiling nervously. "Richard Gotthardt."

A collective gasp was heard from the congregation. One woman on the other side of the room let out a stifled no. I felt the gaze of the people near us watching for a clue of how to respond.

Without looking up, the man standing at the microphone invited Richard to the stage, advising the congregation that Richard had a few words to share with them. This was something the board had asked Richard to do. Essentially they had said, "Hey, we recognize this group of people sees you as their pastor. We don't really want to have a lead pastor anymore, so there's not a place for you here, but would you go ahead and pastor the people through this? And when you're done, we'll no longer be needing your services. Thanks."

Richard had agreed because he was a pastor at heart, not in title.

I let go of his hand as he stood. We didn't make eye contact because we both knew we would cry. But my heart went with him as he moved toward the front of the room. He walked to the podium without looking at the board members. He was up there to do the right thing for the congregation; to honor God and God's church, not to pretend what was happening was right.

As he always did, Richard shared authentically about the loss this was for him. How he knew every crack in the sidewalk. How every major event of his adult life had occurred on that campus. He had met me there. We had married there. We dedicated and later baptized all of our children there. He ministered to thousands of people, led hundreds of college students all over the world, prayed with and counseled countless others. And for years he had tried to be a point of stability in a tumultuous, sometimes chaotic environment—in both healthy and unhealthy ways. And now God was releasing him. And although he didn't know what was ahead, he knew he would be okay. And they would be okay. Then he thanked them for the privilege of being their pastor and left the stage.

The response was instant and forceful—the congregation was on their feet, applauding, some crying. I was a wreck. So full of pride in my husband. Thankful for the opportunity for him to display the character of God that he possessed. Full of angst at the injustice of it all. Grateful to be almost done with this painful evening. Full of regret that we'd not left sooner or on our own terms. More uncertain than ever about this thing we call church.

And this was my year of abundance.

Moving Forward

I can't leave the story there because I feel a sense of responsibility. Perhaps there's still a bit of the dutiful "good girl" in me. And maybe that's a good thing.

My wrestling with God about church began long before the night I've just described. It probably began on that day in the car with Richard. The day I uttered my first beautiful no. Which is the problem with following Jesus—it often leads to places you wouldn't have gone and don't know how to navigate.

And my wrestling continues. But today I'm not wondering if the church is necessary. I'm more convinced than ever that God intends for his people to live out a visible expression of the transformation that is occurring in us and through us. Church is a taste of the ultimate, complete redemption and transformation that will occur when heaven comes to earth on the last day. And it is messy.

Today I'm asking how God is inviting me to invest my gifts to help create more healthy expressions of his kingdom. And I'm not talking about taking a spiritual-gifts inventory to figure out which ministry I can plug into (not that there's anything wrong with that). I'm wondering how I can use my gifts to help others more effectively, authentically, and gracefully live out what it means to be the church in the context in which they live.

How did I get from anger, disappointment, and growing bitterness to forgiveness and passion? That's probably a book in itself. But first let me tell you what I didn't do.

I didn't swallow my anger because I was ashamed of it or thought it ungodly. I didn't pretend everything was fine. I leaned into my anger as I walked through the bramble-filled path of this season. On the other side of the weeds I found I could eventually feel compassion for people from whom I'd experienced hurt. Imperfect people like me who were trying to make life work.

I didn't just wait for the hurt to go away—because I knew it wouldn't go away without some work.

I didn't give up.

I didn't give in to despair.

And by some miracle, I'm passionate about the local church. Not because a good pastor's wife should be positive about church (although I do desire to be my husband's biggest supporter and fan). I'm passionate because my journey toward God led me to this place.

So, what did I do? A lot. I'm fairly high maintenance. And I did not do this alone.

Now is as good a time as any to tell you about my "team of experts." This is the group of people with whom I've surrounded myself that help me stay a healthy, relatively sane, contributing member of society. I don't know how people survive without a team like this.

Let me introduce you. First, there's my friend Carol. She's my self-proclaimed Jewish mother, though she's neither Jewish nor my mother. She is, however, my sounding board, my mentor, my friend, my fellow journeyer, my wise sage.

Then there's my therapist. When I write that, I feel like I'm in a Woody Allen movie, but at this point in my story, you've got to admit I'm a woman in need of professional counseling. I often joke that I've got her number on speed dial. It's not quite that dire, but she knows my story, and even though I pay her to listen to me, I fancy that she likes me. She doesn't let me get away with feeling sorry for myself, and she has been instrumental in the major breakthroughs that have made me a more whole human being. I'm closer to the woman God created me to be because of her.

I've got a spiritual director. This is someone who helps me discern the movement of the Holy Spirit in my life. But even more, it's a place where I go to gain perspective. It's where I get reminded of what matters for eternity, and it's a place where someone speaks my language. I don't have to explain myself. There aren't a lot of places like that in my life, but when I'm with her, I feel like the space between the spiritual world and the physical world is diminished.

There's my chiropractor, whom I like to call my woo-woo doctor. She is a healer, and if I were independently wealthy, I would employ her as my personal masseuse. I don't know all the science behind what she does, I just know that whenever she puts her hands on me, I feel more energized and open. I'm a firm believer in the connection between our body, mind, and spirit, and she is a key part of that for me.

And at different times I've hired a personal coach to help me through a transition or a new experience.

These are just the professionals. I've also got a highly supportive family and a network of friends, colleagues, and classmates whom I regularly reach out to for advice, feedback, prayer, and assistance.

God has worked through each of the men and women I mentioned in unique and personal ways. I would love to share them all, but there are some things that don't translate well to paper. They are so sacred and personal that to speak them robs them of their power.

I've learned to ask, "What is God's invitation in this?" And I have continued to lean into that question. In the midst of injustice. In the midst of pain. In the midst of questioning. In the midst of my own selfishness and immaturity.

In the end, this story isn't about the church—this messy bride of Christ—or my questions of the future. It's about God's redemptive work in the world through all of it. It's intensely personal and profoundly global.

It is abundant. And in me, it's still a work in progress.

CHAPTER 16

The Beauty of Yes

Eventually it had come time to do something. Saying no had opened up a whole new path. But no was never the goal. No simply created space for the best, life-giving yeses.

And this was becoming clear—the tension between no and yes would always be with me. My former self had hoped I could master this tension, finding a formula that would help me create the perfectly balanced life where I was sufficiently productive without ever becoming too tired. It soon became clear this was just another attempt at control. A radical, rebel life sometimes spends itself recklessly in pursuit of justice and love. Like Mother Teresa. Or the many ordinary saints I know who have disrupted their balanced, comfortable lives to take in foster children or care for refugees or walk alongside the broken and discarded members of society. According to St. Augustine, the challenge is to learn "to love—the right thing—to the right degree—in the right way—with the right kind of love."

Yes to Time with God

Discarding my spiritual practices (at least the way I'd understood them) was one of my early rebellious nos. I refused to participate in what felt to me like a rote, formulaic process that kept me intellectualizing my faith. I had come to view it as just another way to earn God's favor and find the keys to a good life. I wanted more of God so I chucked all the other stuff—Bible reading, Bible study, lists of requests, prayer journals—and started from square one. Each day I set a timer for ten minutes and sat in silence in God's presence. Sometimes I did this at the beginning and the end of the day. I gradually began spending fifteen, then twenty, and then thirty minutes in silence in God's presence.

As I continued to journey, I learned that all of this was a natural progression of spiritual maturing. The early ways that help us connect with God were never designed to take us through every season of life. It was normal to desire new ways of connecting in relationship. It happens in human relationships and in spiritual relationships.

I was in no hurry to do anything else. But as I continued to sit in silence with God regularly, my appetite for his Word began to reawaken. About this time I was introduced to an ancient practice of Scripture reading called *lectio divina*. Essentially, this way of meditative reading allowed me to engage my whole self in a conversation with God. I learned to listen and respond. I acknowledged emotions. And not just the "good" ones, like love, joy, and peace. Sometimes I felt "less spiritual" emotions like fear, anger, and confusion when I read the Bible, and I discovered that God wasn't offended or quick to dismiss my concerns and questions.

Some days I would incorporate movement into my time with God. Yoga was such a gift to me as I learned to pray with my body. I practiced prayer using doodling and drawing. As I engaged my left and right brain in the process of prayer I found creativity where I thought I had none. I found deep passions I didn't know existed in me. And I discovered a hunger for God I had once believed would elude me in this life.

And just when I felt I'd reached the perfect balance, holy discontent led me to something new.

Yes to Activity

"I've reached the end of my domestic energy," I admitted to Richard as we relaxed in the living room. "I can only organize closets and plan meals and clean the house for so long. I've got to do something else." I wasn't just talking about that day. I meant "in my life."

Richard nodded his head affectionately. "So, this is as good as it gets?" The reality of my domestic limitations was setting in.

He surveyed our home as he smiled. While comfortable and warm, no one would accuse me of being compulsively neat. His eyes stopped on a pile of books in the corner of the dining room. The books had been there for weeks, and I still hadn't figured out what I wanted to do with them. They were stacked neatly and out of the way, but still . . . weeks? And meal planning was my undoing. So many options, so much time necessary to plan, shop, prepare, present, and clean up. Of course, I did have the time; it's just not how I wanted to spend it. And after years, nay decades, of practice I still couldn't just whip something up with what I found in the kitchen.

I wasn't working. Our kids were all in school. After they were out the door, I often had the whole day ahead of me. Most days I'd sit outside with a cup of coffee, my Bible, and my journal. I had long since given up on studying long passages of Scripture or analyzing the text. On these mornings I would meditate on a verse or two, allowing God's words to breathe life into me or convict me or reveal something deeper in my desires. I often sat in silence, enjoying the presence of God, and I prayed for long periods, effortlessly and freely. I was experiencing life and peace. My cup was full—running over, even.

Others seemed confused and unsure about the spiritual appropriateness of my way of life. There were puzzled looks when women made statements like, "I'm sure you're very busy. . ." and I replied, "Actually, I'm not." Responses to that revelation often exposed thinly veiled anger at my intentional rejection of the unwritten busyness code many of those around me had embraced.

Don't worry, in spite of all the goodness, I often felt guilty for my pace of life. It had been a season of healing from addiction to busyness, compulsive codependency, and activity-based Christianity. For the first time in my life, I felt the joy of simply being.

In all honesty, I wanted to spend more time being. I was afraid of doing. It felt like death. So of course that's where God sent me. Not because he's a sadist, but because he conquers death.

We made the transition from the pain of leaving our former church and joined a group of beautiful friends who'd invited Richard to shepherd them. We were experiencing community in a new and life-giving way, and we both seemed to be healing, ever so slowly. Our kids were settled in new schools and making new friends and I was living life at a manageable pace that allowed time for a deepening relationship with God, spontaneous time with friends, and some mentoring of young women. This was the life I imagined when I first stepped down from my ministry obligations, and it seemed good. But something wasn't right and the disconnect first appeared at home.

With my life running so smoothly, I assumed I would become more organized, better able to manage my household. Budgets would be up-to-date, meals would be simple but creative, and the house would be neat and clean most of the time. Large piles of clean laundry would no longer get folded "as needed." Dirty dishes wouldn't remain in the sink overnight.

What? A girl can dream, can't she?

I did make improvements. But on the day I initiated this conversation with Richard, I felt defeated. I had completed all the projects I had hoped to finish, and the thought of maintaining these routines felt like a slow death. I realized I was not made for this, and I began to consider what I should do.

As I wondered about my future, I attended a silent retreat on the coast of California. I longed to help other Christian leaders find the sanity and soul nourishment I was experiencing, and I assumed God's next step for me would be into the field of spiritual direction or coaching Christian leaders.

As I started my silent retreat on the cool grass in the center of the historic mission courtyard, I began a collage that I thought would depict being. Somehow I found myself gluing the word *do* to my paper. Then . . . *act.* In the midst of all my being words, God was clearly directing me to action of some kind. But what?

I left the retreat confused. I thought I'd misunderstood. I pursued a job coaching leaders, but some wise people around me shared they felt it wasn't a good fit. That door slammed shut.

God waited a month, then showed me his plan as I drove to Home Depot. I don't know why he chose Home Depot as my burning-bush moment, but it has forever changed my experience of home improvement. Regardless, three months later I was working for a nonprofit organization, fully immersed in a world of doing and performing and activity.

The three next years I spent trying to integrate the new spiritual practices I'd learned, the inner calm I'd cultivated, and my growing love for God into my life as a leader. I felt propelled for a purpose—creative, energetic, and resilient. God had clearly put me in this place.

And yet, it wasn't all going well. I was having trouble maintaining the pace required to succeed in my position. As a regional leader I was required to travel and my staff were spread out across two states and four cities. This meant it would take more time for them to trust me and for me to build the kind of relationships in each region that would make growth possible. I was not going to succeed quickly.

It was also an organization in the midst of change. Within the first year, my key staff were all new, as were all of our job descriptions. I was sinking. How could this be? Hadn't God clearly brought me here? Shouldn't that ensure success? Apparently not. Toward the end of my second year, one of the executives pulled me into her office for a casual conversation. As we discussed my strengths (my team was functioning well, I was innovating and developing new ways to meet client needs and improve the product we provided, and I had great relationships with clients) we inevitably had to address the elephant in the room—I was not meeting the agreed-upon measurable results established for my role. My region, while I believed it was getting healthier, was not getting bigger. And that is what I had been hired to do. To top it off, my boss did not believe I was capable of accomplishing what was being asked of me.

I felt hurt and angry. But mostly angry. Angry at God for inviting me into a season of failure. Angry at myself for not succeeding at either one of my goals—success at work and success in integrating my new self into this environment. But as my emotions settled and I asked God what to do, I sensed an invitation to stay.

This was a new place for me. I couldn't recall a single time in my life where I stayed in a place with people telling me "you can't do it." But that's what I did. Instead of quietly slipping out, I stayed engaged. I asked them to give me the fourth quarter to meet my goals and see if I could succeed. I didn't believe it was time for me to be done, and I sensed God had more for me to learn.

As with my year of abundance, I had chosen a theme word for the year. It was faith. I had completely forgotten about it in the busyness and difficulty of the year (negating the supposed purpose of choosing a word), but it seemed now was the time to explore why I had been drawn to it nine months earlier.

I returned home from that meeting and immediately registered a domain name and began a blog. I had seventy-five days until the end of the year and the end of my test, and I titled the blog *My Seventy-Five Day Journey of Faith.* I invited a few friends and family members to come along with me, and I was off.

Journey of Faith

One tiny problem was that I had no plan. Hypothetically, that shouldn't have been an issue because this was a faith journey. But now I was remembering why I had chosen the word *faith* in the first place— because I possessed very little of it. It didn't take an Excel spreadsheet (which I loathed) to figure out the bottom line on this one. I had no track record of meeting my goals, no new plan to even attempt, and no discernible faith that God would come through.

God and I had an ongoing dialogue about the purpose of prayer. When I'd quit having a conventional quiet time, I quit engaging in regular intercessory prayer. Even though I believed the prayers of my mother, grandmother, and aunts had sustained me through the most difficult times, it did not make sense to me. I could say I believed in the power of prayer, but if actions betray belief, I wasn't telling the truth.

I prayed every day. But my prayer was usually without words or focused on praise and thanksgiving, areas I'd long neglected in my youth. So how would I go about living in faith? When I accepted the job, I had decided I would remain true to who I was and the way of living I had been practicing. Without acknowledging it consciously I think I believed God would honor my choices by giving me astounding business results. That had not happened. I could spiritualize it all day long, but the truth was, it wasn't helping me meet my agreed upon goals—even in a faith-based nonprofit.

However, I had no other plan to speak of so I went with what I had.

At our quarterly senior leadership meeting I shared my three-year plan with no hiding my agenda. I described my plan in my blog:

Excerpt from Day 6 of my journey:

> I'm going to tell them what I believe God is inviting me and my team to do and how we believe he wants us to get there. Not with more Excel spreadsheets or better incentives or more motivational speakers or efficient systems (not that those are bad), but with discipleship and eyes on Jesus and ears tuned to the Holy Spirit and with faith and a spirit of adventure and movement forward in joy and peace. With creativity and flow. With courage and integrity. With hard work and intentional rest. Within the context of community for the glory of God . . . "With simplicity and godly sincerity, not by earthly wisdom but by the grace of God."

It's not difficult to see the passion in my plan. But the further I moved along on this experiment, the more I realized I was not being asked to change the organization. I was going to have to make some decisions about how I interacted within a structure I didn't create. Submitting to someone else's authority was proving painful now that I'd grown comfortable with rebellion.

From Day 42:

> Quoting Nietzsche is probably a sure sign of my tendency to overanalyze, but I'm quite proud that I've been able to abstain for 6 weeks. "Whoever fights monsters should see to it that in the process he does not become a monster." Or as Paul said to the Galatians in chapter 6: "Brothers and sisters, if someone is caught in a sin, you who live by the Spirit should restore that person gently. But watch yourselves, or you also may be tempted."

The Nietzsche quote was from *Reading Lolita in Tehran: A Memoir in Books*. The author, Azar Nafisi, is describing how the revolution in Iran made her feel increasingly irrelevant. Having to wear the veil, loving things that were no longer valued, holding on to ideals that made life more confusing, not clearer. Maybe that's the toughest for me—the confusion. Which is why legalism is so attractive. Black and white means no confusion. Everything is clear. This is right; that is wrong. Nafisi describes the dilemma of choosing to teach while wearing the veil and looking like a hypocrite to her students or standing by her ideals and shunning the teaching role and denying students of the knowledge of literature she loved as long as the veil was a prerequisite. In either case, some would call her a traitor. In her words, both accusers would be correct.

I think that's how I feel. Do I give in to a model of expansion that doesn't fit me so I can have a platform to share a life of vitality and healthy rhythms with people who may never hear it? Or do I stand by my ideals and walk away without anything else to take its place? In either case, I fear becoming the monster I am fighting.

Frankly, I only have a vague idea what I was talking about in that post. By this point I was clearly spiritualizing my self-righteousness. But with less than two months to go, the real purpose in this faith experiment began to come into the light.

From Day 51:

> On Sunday, Richard read a prayer from John Wesley on surrendering each day to Jesus. One line read: "Employ me for you or lay me aside for you." If I work, let it be for you. If I'm let go, let it be for you.

In life it is easy to let go of the main thing. Even in my seventy-five-day experiment I found it hard to stay focused on what I was trying to accomplish—an increased faith. But before I was given a new dose of faith, I was reminded of my own frailty.

From Day 62:

> Moving forward in faith has shown me more ugliness in myself than I had hoped for. I was going for more of a "Chicken Soup" experience of faith and I'm getting a spiritual overhaul.

Feels suspiciously like a bait and switch. God invites me into this journey of faith—"Watch me work." Sounds good to me. I could use some inspiration. I'll even put some effort into it (very noble of me). Before I know it, I'm being shown some less-than-inspiring sides of my personality and leadership style. Wait a minute! When did this become about me?

This feels very much like the time I brought Richard to marriage counseling to help him stop being angry with me and I left realizing I was trying to control his emotions. I still don't know how that happened!

My need to be understood and affirmed, my issues around money, and my attachment to a particular view of success have all been called out this week. That's a lot of dirty laundry to sort. I've been irresponsible, reactive, and manipulative at times. Of course, I do it in a very likable way, but when viewed in light of God's Word, it doesn't escape the sword.

What I'm learning about any journey that God calls me to is that there will be pain. Not because God is mean, but because I make mistakes. The more closely I walk with God, the more evident my own shortcomings become. This is inevitable and good. And hard. This is always the invitation. "Come to me . . . walk with me . . . be transformed."

So I guess it's less of a "bait and switch" and more of a "buy one, get one free." Sign up to increase my faith and become more like Jesus in the process.

Somehow, in the fertile soil of small amounts of skill, no plan, and an anemic faith, I accomplished the required goals by the end of the year. Actually, it certainly wasn't me, but the goals were accomplished. I'm still not sure how it happened. And as I reflected on the process, I was amazed at my own transformation.

Day 82:

My journey has come and gone, and writing about it has saved me. Had I not written down these thoughts, I would have been tempted to downplay the process. I would have chalked it up to being dramatic or overanalytical. But the truth is I am a different woman as a result of the journey. While today it feels like it was easy, the pages of this journal reveal a different course. Ups and downs and unanswered questions and discouragement and fear and small victories and painful self-realizations.

Ultimately, I still have my job. And I like it even more. But I will go about it differently because I am different.

Later that month I sat across the table from my boss, and he looked at me in puzzlement. "What changed in you? You're completely different from last year." I hadn't invited him to read my blog, so I attempted to explain it as best I could.

As the year progressed I became aware of an internal discontent. A longing for more freedom to contribute in a way that was better suited to my passions and giftedness. And in August, at another silent retreat, I had a dream I believed was a warning.

The Dream

In my dream I cut off a small portion of one of the fingers on my right hand. I found it to be a minor inconvenience and resolved to do nothing about it. But the next day, the clumsiness I experienced as a result of my damaged finger caused me to cut off the pointer finger of my right hand. This was a much greater loss. But I was busy. There were many things I needed to accomplish.

I still had the finger, but I didn't have the time to deal with it immediately. A number of days later I made the trip to the doctor so he could reattach my severed pointer finger. But he simply shook his head as I described my predicament. He told me it was too late to do anything. If I had come to him immediately, he could have saved it, but with all the time that had passed, it was too late. I would have to live without the finger. I was overwhelmed with shame and regret. How could I have been so foolish as to wait?

As I sat with the dream I sensed there was a part of me that was being cut off. Particularly in my role at work. I was ignoring it because I was too busy and it wasn't really keeping me from being productive. I sensed that if I continued to operate without using the best parts of who I was, I would lose even more of myself. And if I didn't do something about that soon, it might be lost forever. I sensed my time at this job might be coming to a close. But before I took action, I waited to get more clarity from God.

CHAPTER 17

The Spirituality
of the Dance Floor

As the music pounded and the strobe lights flashed, I yelled across the table to my friends, "No. You really don't want to see me dance."

Conversation was difficult in this environment, and I was content to sit quietly and observe the action in front of me. These women, however, seemed intent on engaging me and were fairly committed to getting me on the dance floor.

The menagerie of middle-aged bodies mixing various levels of skill with early stages of intoxication made for an entertaining evening. In the movies, dancing in Vegas always seemed more . . . coordinated, attractive. But reality was a cruel companion, and I hated to be the one to break it to them.

Six months after I successfully regained the confidence of my organization, I was busy maintaining my success. As I waited for God to show me what might be next, I did what any truly spiritual person does—I headed for Vegas.

I had been working a trade show booth at a national convention all day, and I was ready to unwind. I was tired of trying to convince people of the value of our services and I wanted to go back to just being friends. This was an invitation-only party, and an industry friend had gotten me a ticket. There was no room for work here, and I was in my element. My good friend Amy approached the table where I sat comfortably. I knew I was in trouble. She would not let me sit quietly on the sidelines as an observer. She wanted a dance partner, and truth be told, I wanted to be invited, even though she was a much better dancer than I. She grabbed my hand, and I pretended to resist. I was nervous because, unlike most people on the dance floor, I was aware of my poor skill. I had seen videos of myself dancing at weddings.

In some particularly disturbing footage, I was filmed from behind. I was wearing a sleeveless dress, and my back arm fat seemed to be dancing to a separate tune, syncing to a beat just slightly off the established rhythm. Yet in my head, I felt like I was pretty good.

Amy and I joined a circle of friends already dancing. I couldn't keep from smiling. I knew I looked ridiculous, but I was having so much fun. As I looked around, I was thrilled to realize how many people there I counted as friends. I enjoyed these people, and I was thankful for their place in my life. I wasn't unaware of the drama going on around me—competition, affairs, gossip, etc.—but I was thankful that God had placed me smack dab in the middle of the mess.

One of my clients danced past me. He was with his wife, but he stopped to yell in my ear as I danced. His words made me pause. "You're not like any pastor's wife I've ever known!"

The statement went straight to my core. Oh, that's right. I'm a pastor's wife.

What would Richard think if he saw me here tonight? I knew he wouldn't enjoy this environment. I was certain he'd be squirming at the sight of my uncoordinated dancing.

Part of me was thrilled at my client's affirmation. I wasn't a stereotypical pastor's wife—although I knew there were many more like me—and I hoped it would give him a different picture of Christianity. But part of me understood I might be perilously close to being irreverent.

Twenty years earlier I'd heard a similar assessment of my behavior in a parallel context: "You're really different than I expected you to be." I was reclining on a couch in the sparsely furnished apartment of some male acquaintances. All of us had attended high school in the same small town in Iowa, but to call them friends would have been a stretch. They were older than I, and they attended the public school. I was a Christian-school kid, and while I had friends from both schools, these were not the kind of public school kids I hung out with. Except the young man I was sitting next to on the couch. We had a brief dating stint a few years earlier, but in a rare moment of strength, I called him out when he tried to kiss me because I knew he was still spending time with his ex-girlfriend. That had ended our little fling and spared me what was certain to be ongoing drama and heartbreak.

None of us was in high school anymore, and he had moved with some buddies to Phoenix, where my family happened to be vacationing over the Christmas holiday. On this, the last night before I headed back to college in Minnesota, I had snuck out of the house I was staying in and met up with this questionable group of relative strangers. They met me with a bottle of wine. They wanted me to know they thought I was classy and didn't want to insult me with beer. How thoughtful.

Now I sat in their living room at 3:00 a.m., drinking my glass of wine while they puffed on cigarettes and reminisced about old times in Iowa with each other as if I wasn't there. The presence of someone who knew their hometown and their former glory seemed to be all they needed as they fell into a melancholy stroll through a past life when they were star athletes, regularly featured in the local newspaper, and applauded as they entered restaurants on game day. At one local eatery, their pictures had graced the paper placements on the tables. They had been local heroes.

That reality had come and gone. I imagine a move to the big city had seemed exotic to those back home. Most of their friends remained trapped in a sad sort of no-man's-land between high school and adulthood, living at home, working at the factory, and hanging out at all the high school parties. At least these boy-men had taken a step into something outside that little world.

My presence in this apartment had no redemptive undertones. I was there to escape my life, and I was thankful for the relative anonymity. But apparently I was not an unknown to them. I should have realized there was no hiding in a small town.

It was into this scene that one of the boy-men spoke. I picked up a hint of disappointment as he made the observation, "You're really different than I expected you to be." But it was the follow-up statement that cut through the tipsy fog in my mind. "I heard you were, like, a total Christian."

For all of the nearly twenty years of my life I had labored tirelessly to manage my image. Even when I hung out with "bad boys," they viewed me as a good girl who was just letting off a little steam. In that moment, I realized that no one really wanted me to stop being a good girl. There was hope in the existence of people who had not given in to the futility and emptiness they were experiencing.

But more damaging by far was the indictment on my soul. In all the years of my life, no one had questioned my faith. That godless wanderer had spoken truth, and it both cut into my soul and wrapped itself around me like a suffocating blanket.

Twenty years later on the Vegas dance floor, I was a completely different woman. Yet could I really be considered holy as I jumped and contorted (poorly, I might add) to the sounds of today's pop music? How far I had come from those shame-filled days. But was this where I was supposed to be? And was I allowed to be enjoying it so thoroughly?

I was learning that often activities I engaged in post-transformation were similar to activities I engaged in pre-transformation, but I did so with the freedom that came with a wholly renovated heart. This made external measurement of my spiritual condition more difficult for others.

In many ways, life was simpler when dancing and drinking and hanging out at parties were forbidden. No one could call my behavior into question when I was following the agreed-upon guidelines. I could never be the cause of disillusionment or stumbling to another, and I would surely safeguard myself from the numerous pitfalls inherent in these activities.

The other option was to attend these things and remain piously aloof. I recalled a scene from decades earlier when Richard and I had been invited to play volleyball with his coworkers. It was early in our marriage, and he was working as a juvenile probation officer. It was before the days of full-time ministry when most interactions were with other people who believed the same way we believed. But we were heavily involved in our church, and most outside-of-work activities revolved around those responsibilities and that circle of people.

Richard enjoyed the men and women he worked with. He shared much in common with them, and he admired them. They hung out with each other, but we were busy and had friends. Christian friends.

One day, these people from work invited us into their circle. They approached Richard with a request to join them for their weekly happy hour and volleyball. Now this was a problem.

We would be going to a bar. For happy hour. We discussed it for a long time. Because that's who we are and what we do. We overanalyze things. This was outside the boundaries of our leadership agreements at church. There were rules about drinking and hanging out at bars, and we considered asking them to play volleyball at church with us sometime. In the end, by God's grace, we decided to participate without drinking. We knew it was a risk because if someone from church saw us there with people who were drinking, they might assume we were drinking as well. And then . . . well, who knows what could happen?

What I remember from the night of volleyball with Richard's coworkers was how stiff I was. I wasn't there to enjoy myself. I was there to be a witness. I fear they picked up on the vibe that I was simply gracing them with my presence. I was uncomfortable and properly pious. More accurately, improperly pious. I'm pretty sure Jesus was less pious than me because the only people he offended were the religious people.

I certainly didn't have any fun at the volleyball outing. I wasn't supposed to. It was strictly utilitarian—for the purpose of winning souls for Jesus. As a Christian I believed I wasn't allowed to simply enjoy an activity for the sake of enjoying it.

But here I was on the dance floor. Among the people I counted as friends were a group of women who lovingly called me their moral conscience. I had reluctantly invited them along on a six-week journey of self-discovery I was conducting with some other women. They were looking for something meaningful, and I was already planning on leading this study, so against my better judgment I invited them. I adequately warned them that it was a workshop with a foundation of Christian spirituality, and they seemed unfazed.

They brought amazing appetizers and snacks each week and fully participated in each session. In one particular exercise, they were asked to write a prayer based on a number of passages from the Bible. They didn't even blink. They loved it. After having these verses read to them with their name attached, one of the women remarked through tears, "If I'd heard some of this as a child, I'd be so much less screwed up right now."

I found myself drawn to these women as friends and colleagues. I enjoyed being with them, and while I cared deeply about their happiness and the condition of their souls, I just liked being with them. The more time I spent with them, the less simplistic my answers to life became.

In fact, their questions often became my questions. On one occasion I was enjoying a latte with an atheist friend. I liked spending time with her. She was my friend. She shared some deep questions about how to define whether or not she was a good person. Her points were sincere and well thought out. As I listened, I felt able to relate to her pain.

When she spoke, I could easily formulate in my head the "correct" response. The "spiritual" response. But I knew that God just wanted me to listen. I could relate to her angst. I was willing to let the question sit, even as she acknowledged to me that she and her atheist friends were not a happy group of academics.

I thought of my former self and how I would have pounced on this statement. Just a few years earlier, I would have used that statement against her. Today I just loved her. I could see that she wasn't searching for all the answers to her questions as much as for friendship, and I was searching for the same thing.

Yet I have questions. Am I doing enough to point people to Jesus?

A number of years ago, I was spending the day with a development coach. Eddie's job was to introduce me to men and women who might want to support our nonprofit. The whole affair had me wanting to take a shower after each meeting as I made small talk and smiled and tried to give them the answers they wanted to hear.

We went to lunch at a swanky joint in a large city, and I excused myself to use the restroom. I did have to pee, but I also needed to massage my face muscles to endure another hour or so of smiling and expressive conversation.

When I exited the restroom, I spied my coach engaged in a conversation with our waitress. She was clearly trying to walk away without appearing rude or negatively affecting her tip. As I approached the table and slid into my booth I tried to give her a sympathetic smile.

"If you're going to live with him, you need him to marry you," Eddie was advising. "And you should find a church," he added with a grandfatherly touch on her hand.

"Oh, my gosh," I muttered under my breath. I was gone for three minutes. How did he get to this level of intimacy already? I knew I shouldn't have let him out of my sight. Then I felt a wave of relief as I realized I would have had to watch the whole thing go down had I been sitting here, and I felt a tinge of guilt about the joy I was experiencing.

Our waitress laughed nervously and, wisely, chose not to respond to his comment. She turned quickly to grab our check and probably take some calming breaths, and Eddie turned to me with a satisfied grin.

"It's just amazing how these opportunities come up when you're looking for them," he mused. "Life is so short, and I just couldn't let her go without encouraging her to go to church."

He was right, of course. Life is short. There is a God who wants to reveal himself. I happen to know that God. And I knew that even as awkward as that conversation had been, God could use it in the life of that waitress.

I'm grateful for men and women like Eddie who overcome their fears and nervousness to intervene in the lives of others. But I also know I will probably never have that conversation with a stranger. In spite of my poor skills, I am more suited for life on the dance floor.

CHAPTER 18

The Image of God

"Who represents more the image of God, men or women?" The colorfully adorned women in the audience looked away from me and toward the interpreter standing next to me, who asked the same question in Kimeru, the language of this Kenyan region. I wasn't sure how they would respond. On one hand it seemed like an obvious trick question. I had just read Genesis 1:27 to them.

> God created humanity in God's own image,
> in the divine image God created them,
> male and female God created them. (CEB)

On the other hand, I knew that even in the modern world where I resided, the idea of a woman being the image of God was not often discussed. God's image as a human, yes. But as a woman? That was a little less comfortable.

So I waited. They smiled when they heard the question in their own language. I was shocked at the immediate and unanimous response—"the man." There was no hesitation and no question. Obviously the man was more a picture of the image of God.

I asked it again in a different way. "So, you're saying that we, as women, do not reflect the image of God as much as men do?" Once again they responded with hearty affirmation.

I read the passage aloud again—many of them read along in their Bibles. "Where does it say that women are less the image of God? It says here that men and women are created in the image of God. What does that mean?"

I was not trying to start a new feminist movement in rural Kenya. I wasn't talking about the role of women in the community or the church or in their marriages. I simply wanted them to hear the truth that they were equal image-bearers of God. Or maybe I wanted to tell myself.

As a girl growing up in the church, I got some confusing messages about what it meant to be a female image-bearer of God. I'm aware that children often internalize messages that grown-ups never intended to send, so let me share my perceptions. You can be the judge.

I have a wonderfully strong mother. Her story should be told in another book, but watching her gave me an internal sense of my strength. She was an entrepreneur, starting a preschool in our basement when I was four years old. She was a leader in our church, and she passionately pursued Jesus. She was not intimidated by the college professors and theologians who were part of our church family, even though she came from humble roots. She attended a one-room schoolhouse that looked to be straight out of an episode of *Little House on the Prairie* and had grown up poor and somewhat sickly in rural Iowa. I didn't realize as a young girl that she was breaking the rules, so I believed this was just what a woman did.

But there were other messages as well. Not exclusively from my mom. It was simply the culture and the time in history. When a woman signed a check—and this was way before debit cards, so they signed checks all the time—she didn't sign her name. Instead of signing a check as Shirley Kredit, my mom identified herself as Mrs. Jim Kredit. She did this happily.

When we would go shopping together, she would try on an outfit and sometimes fall in love with it. I would watch as my mother viewed herself in the three-way mirror with admiration. I could tell she felt pretty. Yet sometimes when I asked if she was going to purchase it, she would reply, "No. Your father doesn't really like this style." That made no sense to me. I was pretty sure my dad wasn't taking the same thing into consideration. He walked around in his underwear every morning, and none of us wanted to see that. Yet he wasn't asking for our opinions.

The more troubling messages came from outside my home. It began during the first weeks of high school. As freshmen in a high school, we were all expected to participate in a school sanctioned Initiation Day. This day was supposed to help us feel a part of the larger community. Or so I assume that was their intention. Because we were a private school, students came from a number of different rural communities. Most of us had come from very small elementary schools, and consolidating into one larger (albeit still relatively small and rural) school was a bit intimidating.

With any luck, this was the tail end of this tradition because what I experienced in no way helped me connect to my fellow classmates or to the larger student body. And even as I write about it today, I cringe at the blatant sexism, racism, and general inappropriateness of the entire spectacle.

Here's how it went down. On this day every freshman became the slave of a senior of the opposite sex. Yes, we were called slaves, and our assigned senior was called our master. Yes, we had to address them as "Master."

My master's name was Doug. He and his buddies had managed to secure a group of my friends as their slaves, and they outfitted us with harem costumes for the day. That's right. At my Christian school it was completely appropriate for us to be considered sex slaves. It was all in good fun. At the school-wide assembly at the end of the day, me and my fellow harem members were paraded in front of the rest of the student body while our "masters" held up numbers ranging from one to ten, indicating our attractiveness. We were then asked to lie down on the floor while our masters attempted to pour chocolate syrup into our mouths from atop a ladder. No sexual imagery there.

Ironically, in other areas the school was legalistic and protective. We were not allowed to dance, so instead of prom, we had a banquet. Dancing might lead to sex. Apparently sex-themed activities were restricted to school hours.

I was on the drill team that performed at all home basketball games. It was like a dance team, but without the cool factor. We wore long-sleeved white tuxedo shirts with black bow ties atop our homemade, pleated skirts. At the homecoming game we performed our routine in the dark and used glow sticks to create our own low-tech light show. There was some concern that our song choice and hip movements might get out of hand if left unsupervised, and we were regularly visited by a censorship committee. I doubt that was their official title, but that's how we referred to them. On one November evening our choreographer informed us this committee had determined one of our songs could possibly be interpreted in a sexual way so we would not be allowed to use it. Where were these people when I was getting chocolate squirted in my face by my school-appointed master?

But it was at church during college that I learned my sexuality was something to fear and my gender would require me to navigate a delicate balance of competence and helplessness. I could be attractive, but not too attractive—lest I become a stumbling block. Friendly but not too friendly—lest I appear flirtatious. Intelligent but not too intelligent—that could be intimidating. Assertive but not too assertive—lest I be perceived as angry and pushy. A leader, but only where appropriate.

It seemed I was both too much and not enough. Being the "good girl" that I was, I believed these things were true, and I learned to operate within that system.

Then I entered the corporate world. It was hardly perfect, but from the very first day, I knew there was no position unavailable to me. Technically, at least. As a young woman I did get patted on the head by some of the old, established, boys' club members who thought I was sweet. And back in the day, I certainly was sweet.

That's something I lost as I began to shed my good-girl baggage. No one referred to me as sweet anymore. Thank God.

But that's not my point. My point is that when I was treated condescendingly in the corporate world, it was called out as inappropriate. The people who were investing in me were intent on developing me to my full potential.

I found my niche in the Training Department, first training new hires and customer service employees. But soon I was developing the company-wide customer service training program. After that I moved into leadership development. I was developing and presenting training plans to the president of the company. I was helping executives improve their speaking skills. I was managing a team of trainers and operating as an internal consultant for other departments within the organization. I was affirmed and valued. People saw potential in me that I didn't know I had, and I was thriving.

Meanwhile back at the church, I didn't want to be a leader. It wasn't that I didn't lead; it's just that I didn't really like it. I never fully gave myself to it, and it was never something that was uniquely mine.

I sometimes sang up front. I occasionally mentored women. At times I took the leadership training material I was developing in the corporate world and offered it to lay staff at church. I spoke to women's groups. Against my better judgment, I would occasionally speak in the college group if Richard was gone.

Ironically, the one occasion I remember doing this, my topic was submission. My husband is a wise man and he felt this very touchy subject deserved to be delivered by a woman. He recognized women were sick of hearing men tell them they should be submissive. Seemed a bit self-serving, no? And even though I believed that a wife should be submissive to her husband, no one who knew me thought I was just going to do whatever Richard said or assumed I was waiting on him hand and foot.

I spent some time researching the passage, even looking into the Greek word usage. I learned it was a military term that had the imagery of a "voluntary placing oneself underneath authority." I decided to emphasize that.

We met in a fairly new building on our church campus. This room was an amphitheater with rows of chairs set up facing the stage. At that time, about three hundred college students gathered in this low-lit venue. As I stood in front of these young men and women, I couldn't see them very well due to the dimmed house lights and bright stage lighting.

I remember two moments about this talk very distinctly. The first was somewhere near the beginning of the message when I realized I didn't really believe what I was saying. I understood that submission was a biblical term. I believed that submission to God and others was part of my life as a follower of Jesus and that it was especially important in a marriage relationship. I just didn't think it meant what everyone around me said it meant. And practically, Richard and I didn't function in a way that put me below him. I felt like a hypocrite and a fool. I wanted the morning to be over.

It got worse from there. As my eyes adjusted to the low lighting, I had a sense that people were laughing and whispering. Not everyone, but there was a group of guys up in the left corner who seemed to be distracted. As I was making a mental note of this, I heard myself say for maybe the fifth time, "Like I said, this kind of submission does not mean I'm less than my husband, it is simply voluntarily placing myself underneath him." I talk with my hands so I made a motion to demonstrate this concept (as if it were a difficult one to grasp) with my left hand underneath my right.

It was the equivalent of a middle school P.E. teacher saying, "Everyone go grab your balls." Only it was in church, and the pastor's wife was saying it repeatedly.

I never agreed to speak in the college group again.

Through the years I figured out a few rules for how to navigate my way around the male-saturated world of ministry.

Number one: Communicate like a man—be concise, use bullet points.
Number two: Be careful never to be labeled an angry woman—that label sticks.
Number three: Be assertive enough to demand respect, but in a non-confrontational way.
Number four: (I stumbled on this one by accident) Lead in a para-church organization.

In 2010, I became the regional vice president for a national ministry. It was the first time I had ever worked in full-time ministry. And this really didn't count. It was a faith-based nonprofit that operated a business. I anticipated that I would thrive in the industry side of my role. That had always been my forte.

What I found was I loved meeting with pastors. Well, not all of them. But very often I left a ministry meeting feeling energized and full of ideas. I wasn't on a church staff and was operating in a business setting, and they seemed open to collaborating with me. I loved hearing about what they were doing and encouraging them whenever possible. I had years of experience in both ministry and the corporate world, and I was full of excitement about how we could partner.

I began attending a monthly gathering of local pastors, and although I wasn't in church ministry and that was the subject matter, I soaked it up. I loved listening and learning. And I had plenty of ideas of my own. That puzzled me. I thought I disliked ministry.

Then one day, in a conversation with a friend, I heard myself say, "I think I'm a frustrated church leader." And there it was. In spite of my angst and pain and apparent distaste for ministry, it explained why I couldn't stay away, why I continued to share my opinions, and why I spent my spare time reading about ministry and thinking about forms of church community.

This realization created more questions than answers, but it also changed my course. I had never let myself dream about what leadership in the church might look like for me and it frightened me. It also unlocked a hidden garden of ideas and possibilities. I didn't have to hand over all my ideas to someone else, but I could collaborate with a team of like-minded leaders who were working together. I don't know what this looks like, and it is somewhat unconventional in my world, but it helps to know what's inside me. To know what is possible and what my passion is.

Last summer at a ministry retreat I was attending, one of the facilitators was a woman who had served on the pastoral staff of a large church and is an author and a church consultant. She spoke very graciously about the issue of women in ministry. To end her time, she divided us into groups of four. Each group had three or four men and one woman, which frankly is a high ratio of women at an evangelical ministry gathering. The assignment was for the men to listen to the women about what it was like to be a woman in the church.

It's not every day that I'm asked to stand up and pick a group of men, but that's what happened. These guys didn't really know me. And when I'm first engaging in a new ministry context, I may initially seem sweet. I smile a lot, and I'm friendly. I don't know how they viewed me, but I'm quite sure they weren't expecting what they got. I know I wasn't.

It was a comfortably warm, humid day in Nashville, and we were near

Vanderbilt's architecturally stunning campus with the stability of stone buildings covered in ivy, the natural beauty of blossoming peach trees, and the smell of freshly cut grass. There is something welcoming about the landscape in this part of the country. Something that invites you to sit down under a sprawling tree, take off your shoes, sip some sweet tea, and shoot the breeze.

My four men and I found a round table outside and situated ourselves around it. For one of the few times in my twenty-five years' experience in church ministry, I was being listened to by four church leaders. They were gracious and listened well, and it became more of a dialogue than a monologue. One of the unsuspecting men began to share about the difficulties of working with women. Nothing difficult about their skills or abilities.

No, just that "he knew himself" and was afraid of the temptation. He was being very vulnerable with this group of near strangers. It was a confession of sorts, although it was more of a resignation to what seemed to him to be the unfortunate reality.

And today, I was not accepting that reality.

As he spoke I felt my face turning red as my heart began to race. My breath was shallow and erratic as the all too familiar lump in my throat rose up. I opened my mouth, expecting an audible sob or frustrated sigh to escape. Instead, I heard myself speak.

Not speak, really. Closer to a yell, I responded with an intensity that surprised even me. Out of my mouth came a phrase not said by good girls. A very bad two-word phrase. One of the worst.

And time stopped.

"You're better than that!" I continued. I was nearly yelling now as I experienced both anger and sadness at the helplessness he felt.

And I was crying. Such a girl.

I'm laughing as I think about their expressions. They appeared to cease breathing. I've noticed that often men freeze when women cry. Especially strange women. And then when a Christian woman, who up until that point has appeared to be virtuous, godly, and externally put together breaks out with some rather startling language . . . well, that's a lot to take in.

But these were exceptional men and we were experiencing an unexpectedly sacred moment.

Almost as powerful as my outburst was the realization that I was holding a deep pain. Those words came from somewhere. From a part of me that had been waiting a very long time to spit them out. It probably sounded funny or cute or just odd (remember, I'm the girl who couldn't repeat even mildly coarse language without people snickering), but the surprise factor and the force of emotion with which it was delivered kept them from laughing. And, the holy sense that healing was happening in a most unlikely manner. And not just in me.

The man on whom I'd just unloaded looked at me with sincerity. "You know what? You're absolutely right. That is lame. I am better than that." There was a new calm in his demeanor and it almost seemed he was relieved.

One of the other men shook his head. "You need to meet my wife." I get that a lot.

And another described his own anger at thinking that his young, talented, competent daughter might be limited in ministry because she was a girl.

The five of us talked for a while. We laughed. We affirmed each other. We hugged. It was nice. And on that afternoon, the dark cloud of anger surrounding my own experiences of condescension and objectification disintegrated into a wisp and was gone.

There are still days when the clouds start to gather. If there is one enclave where I find my inner dragon ready to devour my heart of love, it is here. The subtle belittling, objectifying, and scandalizing of women, particularly in the name of spirituality, will severely test my newfound freedom. But I no longer question whether or not I am a co-image-bearer of the Divine.

Back in the tin shed on the Kenyan countryside, I directed the women to read the passage from Genesis again. Then I asked them where it said that men were created more in the image of God than women. Their eyes grew big as they at first smiled timidly. Then they began to comment to each other and soon they were giggling like school girls. These majestic, resilient, resourceful women were beginning to believe the truth of who they were. This did not make them angry at men or power hungry. It produced joy and freedom and a lightness of spirit that brought tears to my eyes.

For years before, and even more since my outburst in Nashville, I've had the privilege of journeying with and learning from diverse, godly, competent, humble women leaders. Women who don't define themselves as "women leaders." They're just leaders. And they're working with men who see them as such. By God's grace I am getting to live that out in a number of settings.

And I am leaning into love. Truth—for sure. Being a voice for justice and change—yes. But I am created in the image of God and with that comes dignity and love for all those who share that image.

CHAPTER 19

Extravagance

California was the stuff of dreams for me as a young woman. I didn't give much thought to it prior to my teen years, but as puberty hit, the idea of spending long days playing in the sand and sun both intrigued and terrified me. I did worship the sun. But I was a small-town girl from rural Iowa. My name was Kelli Sue. My first job was detassling corn. I wanted to go to California some day, but first I would need a new wardrobe.

High School came and went and still I'd made it no farther than Phoenix—close, but not even close to actually experiencing California. And then came college. My sophomore year I transferred to Arizona State University and, being only seven hours from Los Angeles, our church group planned a trip to Disneyland. Of course I would go, but as the weekend approached my anxiety rose. By this time I'd met people who actually lived in California and they blended in with everyone else. But I feared that in their natural environment their inherent superiority and coolness would be impossible to disguise.

I told no one of my fears, but as we boarded the church van for this monumental journey, I thanked God we would be entering the state under the cover of darkness. Perhaps no one would notice this hick as I tried to blend into the culture. Night would provide me the cover I needed to assess the situation and adjust appropriately or cut my losses and embrace my inferiority.

Imagine my surprise upon crossing the state line in Blithe. For those of you who've not had the privilege of making the desolate trek from

Phoenix to LA via I-10, let me describe it. Well, actually, I've already said it—desolate. Blithe is on the Arizona-California border and the California side looks just like the Arizona side, only probably more expensive. So much for my fears of an alarm being tripped when I entered the state. I'd never heard of a hick meter, but it wouldn't have surprised me.

The next day, in the exposure of daylight, I discovered the truth—nobody was on to me.

Over the next twenty-five years, I regularly made the trip to the Southern California coast. San Diego, La Jolla, LA, and Anaheim became comfortable weekend getaway and family vacation spots. It was always difficult to say goodbye to the ocean, but any thought of living in California was rather quickly dismissed. Who could afford it?

As I write this, I'm sitting in a coffee shop with a view of the beach—a little over a mile from my home. The waves are good today and there are a number of surfers out enjoying the unseasonably warm weather on the central coast. How did this happen? I truly don't know.

On vacation four years ago, as I walked along the ocean in this hippie beach town, I asked God if I could live here. Until that point I'd been sharing with him my hope to someday live on a canal/lake in Arizona. I knew God didn't owe it to me, but I also knew he was aware of my desire and it wouldn't hurt to ask.

In Arizona I ran along one such canal/lake and there was a specific house I had chosen for myself. Each time I ran past it I reminded God of my desire. On one day I was sure God prompted me to ring the doorbell of this home and ask if they might be interested in selling it. I'm not the kind of person who approaches strangers and asks random questions. But on this day I felt like it might be a divine moment. I rang the doorbell, sweaty and out of breath from my run, and waited for someone to answer. A woman about my age opened the door and looked at me quizzically. "I know this is random," I stated nervously, "but I run past your house multiple times each week [not creepy at all] and I'm wondering if you might be looking to sell." This was ridiculous on many levels. First, because I'd been watching them remodel this house for over a year. The chances of them wanting to sell after doing so much custom work were minuscule. Secondly, and fairly key, was the fact that there was no way we could afford to buy this house even if they were selling. But I had a sense that God had invited me to do this so I was hopeful there might be some miracle about to take place.

She smiled graciously. "No. We have no plans to sell." And that was it. Years of wondering if God would arrange it so we could live there were unceremoniously put to rest.

So as I walked along the ocean on the last day of my vacation I felt a longing I'd not allowed myself to dream of until this point. Could I live near the ocean? The first thought that entered my mind was of my younger sister. At the time she lived in Afghanistan. What kind of person asks God if she can live in paradise when her sister lives in a war zone? So I let it go. But not before I walked for a long time soaking in the beauty of creation and the experience of God.

One week later we received a phone call inviting us to Santa Cruz. Six months later we arrived. And it seemed this was the next step God had been preparing me for in my missing finger dream. It was time to let go of my job. As we crossed the California border in our moving van it was like a literal turn of the page. I knew one season was over and a new one had begun.

The move messed with my theology. The first year I lived with a mixture of wonder, guilt, and fear. One day as I ran my usual path along the ocean I noticed whales in the bay. I heard this could happen, but I had yet to experience it. I stopped to stare in awe. I felt overwhelmed with a sense of joy and the palpable presence of God. It seemed he was showing off: "Look at those magnificent creatures, Kelli! I never tire of watching them. I've been waiting to show them to you. What do you think?" But instead of appreciation, I felt guilt. "Why are you treating me so nicely? Why do I get to enjoy this while so many others in the world are suffering?" As if God was unaware of the suffering and somehow less spiritual than me.

On other days, as I grew accustomed to walks in the redwoods and runs along the sea, I would be overcome with fear that this could all be taken away from me. Amazing how quickly gifts turn into rights.

But this isn't about where I live or the circumstances of my life. This is just a temporal reminder of God's extravagant love. The kind of love that meets us in any location and every situation. And it was through this very tangible lesson that God showed me how to open myself up to more of God.

My Stingy God

Through all of my wanderings I found meditation and silence to be my primary means of prayer. Praying for change in circumstances and help for people was confusing to me. I regularly spoke with God about my uncertainty and invited him to illuminate me. What did intercessory prayer really accomplish? God seemed silent.

It's not that I'd never experienced an answer to prayer in my own life. I had. Like the time ten years earlier when I'd been sitting at my dining room table looking at our budget. It was October and my heart sank as I realized we would need $10,000 to get out of debt by the end of the year. That would be impossible. We had started the year debt free and I felt defeated and ashamed. We were stewarding our money more wisely but still had much to learn. A few unforeseen expenses and poor choices later and we were back in debt. I wrote the number in my journal and acknowledged that only God could arrange for that debt to be erased. It wasn't a particularly inspired or powerful prayer. It was more like whining than intercession. I had no expectation my prayer would be answered.

Two days later I received a call for a contract on my consulting services that totaled just over $10,000. One call. Out of the blue. Debt gone.

So God could handle my financial situation. But I didn't deserve the help. Not only did I not have any faith, it was primarily my poor handling of the finances that got us to that point in the first place. I felt embarrassed and guilty. Instead of an extravagant gift, I received it as an under-the-table handout.

I imagined God shaking his head as he looked at me with pity and condescension. "Okay, Kelli. I'll bail you out this once, but you're going to have to do a lot better next time. This isn't usually how I operate—rewarding bad behavior—so don't tell too many people about it. It might give them the wrong impression. I help those who help themselves, right?"

I longed to engage God like the men and women of Scripture—and plenty of friends around me. To pray powerfully for release for the prisoner, sight for the blind, hope for the hopeless. But when I tried to intercede my prayers seemed so small and pathetic, self-serving and impotent. It seemed best to limit myself to prayers of opening myself up to what God wanted for me, not asking him to do something for me or someone I knew.

But God had different plans. He staged a series of interventions that made it impossible to continue on a path of passive prayer.

Intervention 1: A God Who Trusts

One of the little lies that had crept into my thinking was a belief that I couldn't be trusted. I knew my desires were often self-serving and my motives in prayer were often to make my or someone else's life easier and less painful. For this reason it seemed best to let God direct my life and allow myself to experience whatever happened. In reality this was a terribly fatalistic view of God. Even prayers for healing and freedom from persecution were suspect from this point of view.

While reading an assignment for school, I came upon a statement regarding God's trust in humans. His trust in me. I found this to be ridiculous if not offensive. What kind of theological drivel was I being fed? Why would God trust me? I am clearly not worthy of trust. But the thought wouldn't go away. It haunted me and got under my skin. Until finally I mentioned it to my spiritual director so she could assure me I was right.

She listened attentively as I described my outrage at the idea that God trusted me. She verbalized her observation that I seemed quite worked up about the idea and invited me to talk about the strong emotion that accompanied my view. This was not the response I was expecting. I was able to articulate that I didn't know if I could trust a God who trusted me. I was not worthy of trust and it bothered me to even consider that possibility.

She smiled and looked directly at me. "But he does trust you, Kelli."

I wanted to scream but my director's demeanor was so gentle and kind that all I could muster was a louder than usual, "I don't believe that."

In that moment I decided we would have to simply see this matter differently and I would move on to the next topic. Obviously she couldn't help me with this issue. In my mind it was settled—God did not trust me.

A few weeks later I was leading a group of worship leaders through an exercise of listening to God. After sharing a brief history of the practice of silence, some of the benefits of this type of prayer, and some ideas on how to listen in the next hour, I released them to time alone with God. The keynote speaker for this event was Paul Young, author of *The Shack*. The intimacy he shared with Papa (God) and the profound joy and almost unsettling assuredness of his belovedness had already impacted my perception of God. Paul engaged in this time of silence along with the rest of the participants.

I love helping to create space in a person's life to simply "be." A place where performance ceases and the presence of God often permeates in personal ways. But these exercises are always a risk. If God doesn't show up, I have nothing to offer. In these spaces intellectual assent will not do and every time I send a group away to be with God there is a tinge of fear. What if God doesn't show up?

As the participants began to wander into the meeting room at the appointed time, I could see on their faces that God had met them there and I couldn't wait to hear their stories. One of the last people to return was Paul Young and he entered with a large smile on his face. I expected nothing less. As he approached, he handed me a folded yellow note card and whispered in my ear, "Papa gave me a message for you."

Just so you know, that doesn't happen to me every day. But it didn't seem out of the ordinary that if someone were praying for others during a time of silence they might get words of encouragement to share. I was touched, but not amazed. Until I opened the note card and read it. Scrawled on the page was not a generic word of encouragement. It was very personal and very direct.

Tell Kelli that I trust her—Love, Papa

Tears came instantly and my legs buckled briefly. I had told no one of my questions around trust or the conversation with my spiritual director, least of all a near stranger whom I just met the day before. Who is this God who so compellingly enters my world? Who desires to speak to me even when I'm not listening? Who answers questions I don't know I'm asking? And who trusts me?

I pulled myself together to debrief the exercise but I knew I would not pray the same after this.

Intervention 2: Real Life Answers

After God's personal note to me I realized I might be being invited into something new. But what? And was that really real? Maybe I was making too big a deal of the note. Then God intervened again. Six months after the note I was in Israel getting ready to lead a retreat. My colleague and I arrived a few days early to meet with some women who weren't able to attend the gathering and to acclimate to the time change. On one evening I had dinner with a beautiful young woman who shared her story with me. It seems Jesus makes a practice of showing up to people even when they're not looking for him. In this woman's life, he showed up in dreams repeatedly. Even when she begged him to stop. Until she knew he was God and he loved her and she loved him. I had heard of this happening, but I'd never sat with someone and looked into their eyes and known they had seen Jesus. Could it be that God was this personal? This involved? This close? This extravagantly good? And, if so, what did this mean about the way I prayed?

Intervention 3: Asking for Action

The next day when I joined my colleague at breakfast she informed me one of the women would not be able to attend the workshop scheduled to begin in 24 hours. This participant was coming from Palestine and had been denied a visa. It was a done deal. Only, I wasn't quite ready to give up. A week earlier I would have seen this as God's plan and I would have sent my condolences while trusting that this was for the best somehow. But today I wasn't so sure. I knew this retreat would be restful and renewing for her. I believed God had chosen each woman for a reason and I was suddenly emboldened with my own trustworthiness. I believed she needed to be there and I began to pray. I emailed my prayer team back in the States and asked them to join me in asking

God to act. I couldn't remember the last time I'd used this many words in prayer.

The answer came the next day—she was miraculously granted a visa and would be able to attend the retreat. It was the answer I had expected and it seemed strangely normal. Not ordinary, but not out of character for a God of such extravagance and closeness.

So I'm learning to walk with an extravagant God. And, strangely, this God is much more terrifying than the pragmatic God who enjoys sending me difficulty so I can grow. I'm comfortable with pain. I'm aware of my feebleness. Why would the God of the universe want to laugh with me?

I no longer accept the narrative that God is mistrustful or angry with me. I know a Father who not only shows me whales but also makes a way in impossible situations and sends personal notes and appears in dreams and heals sick people and softens hearts of stone. And it's not just me. I see it in my friend Rose Mapendo, who survived life in a death camp in the Congo. She will tell you she has an extravagant God. I see it in my friend Teresa Goines, who started a supper club in San Francisco run by at-risk youth. She has an extravagant God. And I see it in my sister, Heidi, who lives in places most people couldn't find on a map.

I'm learning to live out of this extravagant love and it is one of the most radical things I've ever experienced.

CHAPTER 20

Love

I find this journey of mine similar to walking a labyrinth. A labyrinth is a circular path that winds its way to the center and represents a spiritual pilgrimage, a path of prayer. As I've practiced it, I often carry a concern or question in my heart toward the center and, figuratively, leave it there. I sometimes stand in the center for a few moments, basking in the presence of God, and then I return, reversing the route by which I entered.

The path is usually marked out with small rocks or painted on a surface or embedded in the floor with tile. I'm struck with the inefficiency of walking around in a maze-like circle to get to the center, when I could easily head straight there. That is the Western way. If I am in pain or have a problem or am pondering a question, I look for the most direct route to alleviate the pain or solve the problem or answer the question. The labyrinth acknowledges the time it takes to truly change. It allows me to live with a question without knowing the answer. It encourages me to lean into the pain I'm experiencing, not avoid it or run from it, and to do all of this with Christ as the goal.

When you emerge from the labyrinth, it is from the same place you entered and, in most cases, nothing external has changed. Perhaps little has changed internally—in the short term. I have found that God is at work in the depths, and the journey is never without results. Though often not in the way we measure results.

On the day I first entered the labyrinth of this journey, I took one small step in. I said no. The world I was leaving seemed hostile and exhausting. I longed for refuge and healing, a respite from the confusion and noise I was experiencing. I came seeking healing from burnout. As I began my journey, I felt free and excited to be traveling without the burden of performance-based Christianity. Naïvely, I believed I possessed the map of how the journey would progress, and I intended to soon be exiting with renewed fervor and spiritual vitality.

But as I wound my way toward the center and the heart of God, I discovered much more in my heart that required attention, if I was to be truly free. I hadn't even noticed the plethora of items I was holding on to as I entered, but I slowly let them go as I walked. On some days I would round a corner, certain I had arrived, only to discover I was farther from the center than before. On other days, my burden seemed light, and I walked with patience and ease.

I watched, sometimes with envy, sometimes with pity, as other travelers raced through the maze or scoffed at the whole thing. I kept walking.

Once at the center, I rested. More accurately, God gave me rest. From the center I could see the battles raging outside the labyrinth. I knew I would return to the same world, and I prayed I would be better equipped to live out what I'd discovered about myself and the God who loves me.

I began the long, slow return journey from the center and found it more frightening than the trek in. I had experienced the presence of God and his healing, but I wasn't "fixed," and my world was still messy. On the return trip I had no preplanned map in my head. I was less naïve, but much more trusting. I opened myself up to the work only God could do.

When I finally arrived at the end, or more accurately the new beginning, a miracle had occurred. Without warning, as I looked up to survey the world I had left, the chaos and hate—it had all changed. I saw with different eyes, and what had seemed bleak and exhausting had become colorful and teeming with energy.

In conversations that used to cause my heart to shrink in anxiety and self-protection, I experienced openness and freedom. In situations where I had felt judgmental and superior, I experienced overwhelming love and connection. As the stressors of life compounded, I experienced peace, not fear. Where I had once seen anger and hate, I saw woundedness and fear. Where I had previously felt the compulsion to control, I found I could release and rest.

I had found love.

That's what I found at the other end of this journey. Love. I uncovered the gaping hole in my life that was the absence of love. Being nice was not the same as possessing love. Doing what I was supposed to do was not producing love. It was producing fear. Fear of doing something wrong. Fear of not being able to control my life or other people.

To say that love is the outcome sounds so . . . innocuous. But it is a miracle. The one thing I couldn't achieve through good behavior.

One year after my outburst in Nashville regarding men and women in ministry, I had the privilege of joining those men at the same conference. They each approached me slowly, perhaps afraid they'd rouse the sleeping dragon they had previously discovered beneath my friendly exterior. But that dragon was gone. Or at least shrunken and weak. We laughed and reminisced about the prior year's experience. Much had changed in each of our lives. And each of us had been shaped by that conversation in different ways.

I've not conducted an official survey, but I think most people who know me would tell you I seemed to be a happy child, young adult, and grown woman. After reading the parts of my story I shared with you, you may wonder. But for the most part, I have been authentically friendly and engaging. I have always had an easy smile and two dimples that are getting deeper with age.

That is why I took on what often seemed the very self-indulgent task of chronicling my journey to the center and back. The journey away from being a good girl, where shame and compliance kept me small and quiet, and into the open expanse of love. I'm telling it because it was difficult and it changed me, and it was worth it and I don't want to forget that. But even more, I'm telling my story because I am being redeemed and my Redeemer is good.

Let the redeemed of the LORD tell their story.
PSALM 107:2.

ABOUT THE AUTHOR

Kelli Gotthardt is a writer, speaker, and consultant. She has spent most of her career in the corporate world but has increasingly moved toward nonprofit and ministry work. One of her recent focuses is women's issues, for which she's traveled nationally and abroad, helping women leaders develop life rhythms that increase their capacity to listen, lead, and love. She has a background in training and leadership development and continues to catalyze personal and organizational growth among church and business leaders. Kelli is a frequent blogger, retreat leader, and keynote speaker, and she recently completed her master's degree in spiritual formation and leadership.

She finds renewal in silence, solitude, and exercise—like running, yoga, and paddle boarding on the ocean. She has been married to Richard for twenty-five years and they live in Santa Cruz, California, where he is a pastor. They have three children, two away at college and one at home. You can learn more about Kelli at www.kelligotthardt.com.